DISCARD

HOT AND COLD

BOOKS BY IRVING ADLER

THE CHANGING TOOLS OF SCIENCE
Revised Edition of *The Tools of Science*

COLOR IN YOUR LIFE

DUST

ELECTRICITY IN YOUR LIFE

FIRE IN YOUR LIFE

HOT AND COLD
Revised Edition

HOW LIFE BEGAN

LOGIC FOR BEGINNERS: THROUGH GAMES, JOKES AND PUZZLES

MAGIC HOUSE OF NUMBERS
Revised Edition

SEEING THE EARTH FROM SPACE
Revised Edition

THE STARS: STEPPING STONES INTO SPACE

THE SUN AND ITS FAMILY
Revised Edition

TIME IN YOUR LIFE
Revised Edition

TOOLS IN YOUR LIFE

WEATHER IN YOUR LIFE

HOT AND COLD
REVISED EDITION

By IRVING ADLER

Illustrated by Peggy Adler

The John Day Company
New York

Library of Congress Cataloging in Publication Data

Adler, Irving.
  Hot and cold.

  SUMMARY: Defines the properties and theories of heat and shows how scientists have learned to produce and measure extreme degrees of heat and cold.
  1. Heat—Juvenile literature. 2. Cold—Juvenile literature. 3. Temperature —Juvenile literature. [1. Heat. 2. Cold. 3. Temperature] I. Adler, Peggy, illus. II. Title.
QC256.A34   1974   536   74-9357
ISBN 0-381-99990-4RB

Contents

CHAPTER I

Hot, Cold and Heat

WE USE the words "hot" and "cold" every day, and hardly give them a thought. They seem like such simple words, expressing ideas as plain as the heat of the blazing sun or the chill of a winter wind. But the words are not really as simple as they seem. They hide a deep and difficult puzzle that has fascinated people for thousands of years. The puzzle is, "What is heat, and how does it behave?" Science has solved this puzzle in the last few hundred years, and by doing so has made it possible for us to do strange and wonderful things never seen on the earth before. With the knowledge we now have about heat we can rival nature in making things hot and cold. The hottest thing produced by nature on the surface of the earth is the molten lava that pours out of a volcano. In Kilauea, one of the active volcanoes in Hawaii, the temperature of the lava is sometimes as high as 2200 degrees Fahrenheit. We do better than that in the open-hearth furnaces of our steel mills, where the temperature goes above 3600 degrees Fahrenheit.

On the surface of the sun, the temperature is about 10,000 degrees Fahrenheit. We do better than that in our laboratories, where we can produce a steady temperature of 26,000 degrees Fahrenheit. The interiors of some stars have a temperature of about 50,000,000 degrees Fahrenheit. But we can match this record, too, at the center of an atomic bomb explosion.

We have also been pushing in the opposite direction, reaching lower temperatures than any produced by nature on the earth. In August 1960 scientists exploring Antarctica found that the temperature at Vostok was 126.9 degrees below zero, Fahrenheit. This was the lowest air temperature ever recorded anywhere on the earth. But we have factories that regularly produce a temperature of 310 degrees below zero, Fahrenheit, in order to turn air into a liquid. Scientific laboratories have gone lower than that, to more than 459 degrees below zero, Fahrenheit.

Merely mentioning these temperatures that have been produced by nature and man presents us with another puzzle. If we know these temperatures, it means that somebody must have measured them. But how can we measure temperatures that are so high or so low? The ordinary thermometer you have in your house is made of some liquid mercury sealed inside a glass tube. Can we put such a thermometer into lava to measure its temperature? Obviously not, because a temperature that melts rocks will melt the thermometer, too. Can we use the mercury thermometer to take the temperature of liquid air? We cannot, because mercury freezes solid at about 38 degrees below zero, Fahrenheit. Yet scientists have found ways of measuring these temperatures. They have even found ways of measuring temperatures across great gaps in distance or time. The sun is 93 million miles away, but we can measure the temperature of its surface without leaving the earth. Recently scientists have learned how to measure temperatures that existed far back in the past. They can tell you how warm the ocean was hundreds of millions of years ago, although there were no people alive at the time to see for themselves.

The purpose of this book is to explore these fascinating puzzles, and see how they were solved. We shall begin by noticing some simple properties of heat that you can easily observe in your everyday experience. Then we shall look into the modern theory of heat that helps us understand how it behaves. We shall learn about the methods that are used to produce very high and very low temperatures, and we shall get acquainted with the instruments that measure them.

The Feeling of Warmth

In most bathrooms the water taps are marked HOT and COLD. But even if the taps are not labeled, we can easily tell which is which. All we have to do is turn the water on, and touch it with our hands. We recognize the hot or cold water by the sensation on our skins. This is the first important fact about "hot" and "cold": they are qualities that we can feel. But we must immediately add another fact: we cannot always trust what we feel. To convince yourself of this fact, try a simple experiment. Fill three basins with water, one with hot water, one with cold water, and the third with lukewarm water. Place your right hand in the hot water and your left hand in the cold water, and hold them there for a few minutes. Then plunge both hands into the lukewarm water. You will find that the water will feel cold to your right hand, and hot to your left hand. We certainly cannot trust the

feeling of hot or cold when we get two different sensations from the same water.

Levels of Warmth: Temperature

To understand why the same water feels different to our right and left hands, let us observe a few more common facts about heat. First, we know that there isn't only one kind of hot water. There is hot water that is comfortable to the touch, and is good for a soothing bath. There is hot water that stings. And there is hot water that can give a very painful burn. So we see that there are different degrees of hotness or warmth. If we heat cold water on a stove, the water passes through a gradual series of changes. It changes from "cold" to "cool," from "cool" to "tepid," then it becomes "warm," and later "hot." So "cold" and "hot" are not really different qualities. They are different levels or degrees of the same quality. We call the level of warmth of a body its *temperature*. When we say one thing is cold and another hot, we really mean that one has a higher temperature than the other.

Heat: Something that Flows

We observe next that if a hot and a cold body touch each other, the hot body begins to cool, and the cool body begins to grow warmer. A hot-water bag, for example, placed against cold feet, begins to cool off as the feet warm up. This fact suggests to us two ideas. First, there is something called "heat" that tends to flow from hotter to cooler bodies. We shall discuss what heat is in Chaper II. Second, when heat flows into a body, its temperature rises.

Now we can begin to understand what happened in the experiment. When you place your right hand in hot water, at first the water is hotter than your hand. But then heat flows from the water into your hand, and your hand grows warmer. When you place your left hand in the cold water, at first your hand is warmer than the water, so heat flows from your hand to the water, and your hand becomes colder. When you plunge both hands into the lukewarm water, one hand is warmer than the water, while the other hand is cooler than the water.

Again, heat flows from the warmer body to the cooler one. So while heat flows into one hand, it flows out of the other. That is why the water feels different to the two hands. Our sensation of hot and cold depends on the direction in which the heat flows. A body feels warm to our hands if it is warmer than our hands. It feels cold to our hands if it is colder than our hands.

Heat Flow with Contact

When a warmer body touches or is in contact with a cooler body, heat flows across the boundary between them from the warmer body to the cooler body. This kind of heat flow, between two bodies that are in contact with each other, is called *conduction*.

If a spoon is put into a cup of hot tea, at first the bottom of the spoon, heated by the tea, is warmer than the rest of the spoon. The spoon may be thought of as being made of thin slices of metal that are joined to each other, layer by layer, from the bottom of the spoon to the top. Each layer is in contact with the layer just below it and with the layer just above it. When the bottom of the spoon becomes warmer than the layer just above, heat flows from the bottom to this layer. Then this layer becomes warmer than the next layer above it. So once more, heat flows from the lower, warmer layer to the higher, cooler layer. In this way heat flows from the bottom of the spoon to the top of the spoon, flowing by conduction from layer to layer. This is an example of the fact that heat can flow by conduction *within* one body, from a warmer part of the body to a cooler part of the body.

Heat Flow without Contact

Heat flows to us from the sun, even though we are not in direct contact with the sun. The heat that comes to us from the sun consists of light that we can see and some other kinds of rays that we cannot see but can detect by their warming effect. This kind of heat flow, between two bodies that are not in contact with each other, is called *radiation*.

When a warm body sends out heat radiation, the kinds of rays in the radiation depend on how hot the body is. Your desk, your chair, your own body and the steam radiator in your room send out only invisible rays of heat. An empty aluminum saucepan left over a flame by a forgetful cook becomes "red-hot" and sends out visible red light as well. Before a blacksmith shapes a piece of metal by hammering it, he heats it until it becomes "white-hot," glowing with a white light. The sun is a great ball of gas that is white-hot.

Hotter and Larger

How hot a body feels is a clue to its temperature or level of warmth. But it is not a reliable clue, as we have seen. So it is necessary to find a better one. We find such a clue in a common everyday experience. We sometimes find that a dresser drawer that opens easily in the wintertime begins to stick in the summertime. This may happen because the heat has made the wood swell. Most bodies *expand* or grow larger as they become warmer, and *contract* or grow smaller as they cool off. We have to keep this fact in mind whenever we build something, to allow

for the change in size that comes with a change in temperature. When a mason lays a cement pavement in the city, he makes a series of squares separated from each other by wide cracks. The cracks give the squares room into which to expand when they swell in warm weather. When a railroad worker lays sections of railroad track, he leaves a narrow space between sections for the same reason.

The fact that most bodies expand when they grow warmer gives us a reliable way of measuring temperature. We take advantage of it in the ordinary thermometer that you find in your house. The thermometer is made of a small amount of the liquid metal *mercury* sealed into a hollow glass rod. Most of the mercury is in the round bulb at the bottom of the thermometer. The bulb opens up into a narrow tube inside the glass rod. When the thermometer grows warmer, the glass as well as the mercury expands. But the mercury expands seven times as much as the glass does. It finds the room it needs to expand into in the tube above the bulb. The warmer the thermometer becomes, the more the mercury expands, and the higher it climbs up in the tube. In this way, the height of the mercury in the tube becomes a measure of its temperature.

Why Smoke Rises

The fact that most bodies expand as they grow warmer serves to explain why smoke rises from a fire. The fire warms up the air that is directly above it. As the air grows warmer, it expands. When the air expands, it is spread out more in space. As a result, each part of the

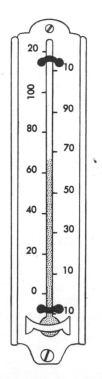

15

space occupied by this air contains less of the air than it did when the air was cooler. This smaller amount of air weighs less than the larger amount of air that occupied the space before. In other words, air becomes *lighter* as it expands. Because it is lighter, it floats upward in the same way a cork does that is released under water. The warm air rises while the cooler, heavier air that surrounds it sinks and flows in to take its place. Smoke rises because it is carried upward by the current of rising air.

Why a Pond Freezes at the Top

Most bodies expand as they grow warmer but there are exceptions to this rule. Water is one of the exceptions. Sometimes it expands, and sometimes it shrinks. This strange behavior of water explains why ponds freeze from the top down.

If a body expands as it grows warmer, it shrinks when it cools. When it shrinks, more and more of the body crowds into a small space. As a result, any fixed volume of the body becomes heavier and heavier. If the body is free to flow, like air or water, the heavier parts sink to the bottom. This happens in a pond when it first begins to cool off in the wintertime. The water at the top of the pond loses heat to the cold air above it. As the water cools, it shrinks, becomes heavier and sinks to the bottom of the pond. So, for a while, the water at the bottom of the pond is colder than the water at the top. However, when the temperature of the water reaches 39 degrees Fahrenheit, a change takes place. As the water cools some more, it no longer shrinks. Now it expands instead. So, once the temperature of the pond falls below 39

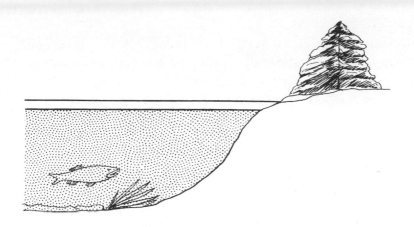

degrees Fahrenheit, the *cooler* water is lighter and floats at the top. Then the top layer of water is the first to be cooled to 32 degrees Fahrenheit, the temperature at which water turns into ice. The ice is lighter than water, and remains at the top of the pond.

Because water expands as it freezes, we have to be careful with our water pipes in cold weather. If water freezes in a pipe, it will swell as it freezes, and may crack the pipe. To avoid damage to pipes that are exposed to freezing temperatures, we drain them before the frosts come.

Water, Ice and Steam

There are three kinds of objects that we see around us. Some are *solids*, like wood, metal, or stone. They hold their shape without the help of a container. Others are *liquids*, like water or oil. They flow freely, and have no fixed shape. They take on the shape of the container that holds them. The third kind are *gases*, like the air we breathe, or the gas we burn in a gas stove. When they are in an open container, they tend to leave it and spread out in all directions. Solid, liquid and gas are often referred to as the *three states of matter*.

In our first experiences with things, we may get the idea that each object has its own natural state. We may think that iron is "naturally" a solid, that water is "naturally" a liquid, and that air is "naturally" a gas. But a careful look around the kitchen will show us that this idea is wrong. When we take water from the tap, it is a liquid. But after we freeze it in the refrigerator, it becomes the solid we call *ice*. And when we boil it in a teakettle, it escapes from the spout in the form of the gas or vapor we call *steam*. Water can exist in all three forms. The state we find it in depends on its temperature. At ordinary room temperature (about 70 degrees Fahrenheit), water is a liquid. At sea level, when water cools, it remains a liquid until the temperature falls to 32 degrees Fahrenheit. Then it changes into solid ice. If the ice is cooled below 32 degrees, it remains a solid. If the ice is warmed, it melts, or turns into liquid again, when the temperature reaches 32 degrees once more. If we make the water warmer, it remains a liquid until the temperature is 212 degrees Fahrenheit. Then it starts boiling as the liquid is changed into vapor, simply getting hotter as more heat flows into it.

There are about one hundred different chemical elements. They are the building blocks out of which all chemical compounds are made. Experiment shows that nearly all elements and many compounds can exist in all three states, solid, liquid, or gas. Air, which we usually see as a mixture of gases, becomes a liquid when we make it cold enough (about 310 degrees below zero, Fahrenheit). Iron, which we usually see as a solid, becomes a

18

liquid if we make it hot enough (about 2800 degrees Fahrenheit). The temperature at which a substance changes from a liquid into a solid or from a solid into a liquid is called its *freezing or melting point.* The temperature at which it changes from gas into liquid or from liquid into gas is called its *boiling point.* Among the chemical compounds, the solids or liquids that cannot change their state when they are heated are those that are changed by chemical action into *different* compounds before they get a chance to melt or boil.

Measuring Temperature

In English-speaking countries, we measure temperature on the Fahrenheit scale, named after a German instrument maker who developed it for his thermometers. The scale is built around the melting point and the boiling point of water at sea level, and the fact that the mercury in the thermometer rises in the tube as it grows warmer. When a thermometer is made, the height reached by the mercury when it is as cool as melting ice is marked on the thermometer and is labeled with the number 32. The height reached when the mercury is as warm as boiling water is marked and is labeled with the number 212. The space between these two levels is divided into 180 equal intervals, and the tops of these intervals are labeled in order with the numbers between 32 and 212. Usually only the multiples of 10 are actually printed on the thermometer. When the mercury in the thermometer reaches up to a certain level in the tube, the number at that level is what we call the Fahrenheit temperature.

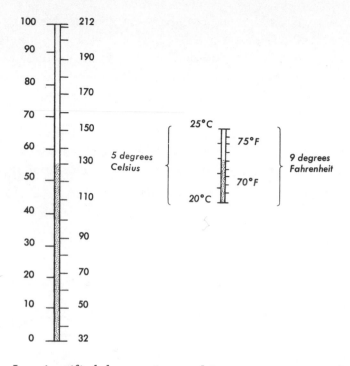

In scientific laboratories, and in most countries of the world, another scale, known as the Celsius scale, is used. On this scale, the melting point of ice is called 0 degrees, and the boiling point of water is called 100 degrees. As a result, a temperature difference of 100 degrees Celsius is the same as a temperature difference of 180 degrees Fahrenheit. We can express the same relationship using smaller numbers: a rise of 5 degrees Celsius is the same as a rise of 9 degrees Fahrenheit. If you know a temperature on one scale, you can calculate the equivalent temperature on the other scale by using these rules: To convert from Celsius to Fahrenheit, multiply by 9/5 and then add 32. To convert from Fahrenheit to Celsius, first subtract 32 and then multiply by 5/9.

20

Heat Flow without Warming

Usually, when heat flows into a body, the body grows warmer. But there are also times when heat can flow into a body without making it warmer. When we boil water on a stove, we find that we have to use heat for two different purposes. First we put heat into the water to raise its temperature. With a fixed amount of water, the more heat we put in, the higher the temperature rises. This continues until the temperature reaches the boiling point. Then the temperature remains at the same level while the water boils. But we have to put more heat into the water to keep it boiling. The more water we boil, the more heat we use up. The heat that flows into the water while it is boiling does not make the water warmer. Instead it changes the water into steam.

In the same way, if we try to melt ice, we find that we have to use heat for two different purposes. First we use heat to raise the temperature of the ice to the melting point. Then we use up more heat to keep the ice melting. Heat may be used to raise the temperature of a body. Heat may also be used to change the state of the body from solid to liquid, or from liquid to gas.

Measuring Heat

These two purposes for which heat can be used give us two ways in which we can measure the *amount* of heat. In one method, we measure an amount of heat by seeing how much it raises the temperature of a fixed amount of water. In the other method we measure the amount of heat by seeing how much ice it will melt or how much water it will turn into steam. In the metric system there is a small unit of mass known as a *gram*. (One pound is about 435 grams.) The amount of heat needed to raise the temperature of one gram of water one degree Celsius is called a *calorie.* This serves as our unit of heat. It takes 80 calories to melt one gram of ice. About 540 calories are needed to turn one gram of water into vapor. Comparing these figures, we see that it takes almost as much heat to melt ice without raising its temperature as it takes to raise the temperature of the same mass of water from the freezing point to the boiling point. After the boiling point is reached, it takes about five and a half times as much heat to make the water evaporate completely as it took to raise its temperature from freezing to boiling.

In English-speaking countries another unit of heat, the British Thermal Unit (BTU), is also used. One BTU is the amount of heat needed to raise the temperature of one pound of water one degree on the Fahrenheit scale. One BTU is the same as 252 calories.

CHAPTER II

Heat and Energy

Warming by Rubbing

IN THE WINTERTIME, when our hands get cold, we can warm them up by rubbing them together. The more we rub them, the warmer they get. This is a simple example of one of the most important facts about temperature: The flow of heat is not always needed to raise the temperature of a body. A body can be made warmer by rubbing it. We have many experiences every day in which an increase in temperature is produced by rubbing one body against another. When an automobile rides over the ground, the rubbing of the tires against the ground makes the tires hot. When you hammer a nail, the nail becomes hot. If you bend a stiff wire back and forth many times, it is like rubbing the wire against itself, and the wire becomes hot at the bend. If you drill a hole in wood, the drill bit may become so hot that it can give you a bad burn.

The Milk Carton That Goes Pop

There are some milk cartons that have a small hinged cover over the spout. There are plastic refrigerator canisters that have them, too. If you have one of these cartons or canisters, remove it from the refrigerator when it is cold and only partly filled, and let it stand on your kitchen table. Be prepared for a surprise. After several minutes the cover over the spout will snap open all by itself with a loud pop. Here is the reason for this noisy behavior of the carton. The carton was only partly filled with liquid, so there was air trapped in the carton in the space above the liquid. Whenever a gas, like air, is inside a closed container, it presses up against the walls of the container. The strength with which it pushes against each square inch of the wall is called its *pressure*. How hard it pushes depends on how warm it is. *The warmer a gas becomes, the harder it presses against the wall of its container.* When the carton was removed from the refrigerator, the air in it was cold. As the carton stood on the kitchen table, heat flowed into it from the warm kitchen air. The air in the carton began to grow warmer, and its pressure increased at the same time. After a while, the increase in pressure was high enough to push the cover open.

We see the effect of warmth on gas pressure in another very common experience. Measure the air pressure in automobile tires before starting out on the road. The usual pressure in properly filled tires is 28 pounds per square inch. After driving for many hours, measure the pressure again. You will find that the pressure has gone up to about 30 or 31 pounds per square inch. The increase in pressure is the result of the ride. We have already seen that the rubbing of the tires against the road makes the air in the tires warmer. As the air warms up, its pressure increases, just as it does in the closed container standing on the table.

Work, a Form of Energy

When you rub your hands together to warm them, you *push* one hand against the other. The warmed-up air in the milk carton described in the last section *pushed* the cover open. A push is an example of a force. A force is measured by the weight it can balance. A one-pound force can balance a one-pound weight. A ten-pound force can balance a ten-pound weight.

When a force pushes something and makes it move, *work* is being done. The amount of work done is calculated by multiplying the strength of the force by the distance through which it was pushing. When a 2-pound force pushes something while it moves 3 feet, the work done is 2 times 3, or 6 foot-pounds.

Work is a form of *energy*. When you rub your hands together you are doing work, and energy is put into your hands and makes them warmer. When the air in a milk carton pushes the cover open, energy is withdrawn from the air as the work of pushing the cover is done. In both cases there is a transfer of energy accomplished by doing work.

Energy Transfer without Work

When heat is conducted from one body to another, or when heat is radiated from one body to another, as described in Chapter I, energy is transferred from one body to the other. But in both cases there is no work being done by a force pushing something through some distance. These facts combined serve as a description of

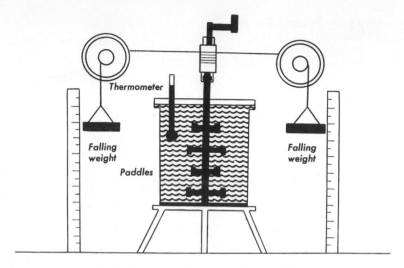

Measuring the mechanical equivalent of heat

what heat is: Heat is energy that is transferred without the performance of work.

Energy, Work and Heat

We live in a world of action. Wherever we look, we see objects in motion. Waves move over the surface of the sea and dash violently against the shore. Water rises into the air as vapor, and then falls to the ground again as rain. The air moves in great currents that we call wind. Living things run and jump and climb. And man-made machines move with swinging levers and whirling wheels. Behind all this action is what physicists call *energy*. The energy may appear in many different forms. Sometimes it appears as work and sometimes as energy of motion.

Sometimes it is hidden, like the energy stored in the position of a weight that is raised above the ground. It may appear as chemical energy or electrical energy. It can also show up in the form of heat, light, or sound. Energy is constantly changing its form, like an actor changing from one costume to another as he plays different roles.

Heat, as one of the forms of energy, can be changed into every other form. And, vice versa, every form of energy can be changed into heat. When a swinging hammer hits a nail, the nail and the hammer become warmer, and then heat flows from them by conduction and radiation. In this way energy of motion is changed into heat. In an automobile engine, heat is changed into energy of motion. In an electric-light bulb, electrical energy is changed into heat and light. In a thermocouple, described in Chapter IV, heat is changed into electrical energy. Whenever these changes of form take place, the amounts of energy that are exchanged have a fixed ratio. Just as one dollar is always exchanged for the same number of dimes (10), or the same number of pennies (100), one unit of heat is always exchanged for the same number of units of work or of electrical energy. The exchange rate for work and heat was measured for the first time in 1843 by James Joule, British brewer and amateur scientist. He used a system of falling weights and pulleys to make paddles turn in a closed container full of water. The churning paddles made the water grow warm just as adding heat to them would, and Joule compared the amount of work that was done by the paddles with the amount of heat that would have the same warming effect. He found that one BTU of heat had the same warming effect as the work done in raising a ten-pound weight to a height of 78 feet, or a one-pound weight to a height of about 780 feet. We call this amount of energy 780 foot-pounds, and it is known as the *mechanical equivalent of heat.*

Chemical Energy and Heat

We get the heat that we use for cooking our food by burning some gas in a gas stove. The burning is a chemical reaction between the gas that flows out of the gas pipe and the oxygen that is in the surrounding air. If the gas is "natural gas" piped up from southern oil fields, it is a chemical compound in which carbon and hydrogen are joined together. When the gas burns, the carbon is separated from the hydrogen, and then each combines with oxygen to form a new compound. The carbon combines with oxygen to form the gas called *carbon dioxide.* The hydrogen combines with oxygen to form water vapor. This reshuffling of chemical elements takes place in the *flame,* and energy is released as it happens. The energy released then flows as heat out of the flame into the surrounding air, or into a pot placed over the flame. This is another example of energy changing its form. When gas is burned, energy stored as chemical energy in the gas is changed into heat that flows out of the flame.

Merely mixing the gas with oxygen is not enough to make it burn. We have to warm it up to its *kindling temperature* first. We warm up a small part of it by holding a lighted match, or the flame of a pilot light, in the stream of gas that escapes from a gas burner when we turn it on. The match flame warms up some of the gas to its kindling temperature, and the gas begins to burn. More cool gas flows out of the burner, but the heat released by the burning gas warms up these fresh batches of gas, and when they reach the kindling temperature, they start burning, too. So the gas burns with a steady flame even after the match is removed.

Burning is only one of many chemical reactions in which energy is released through a reshuffling of chemical elements. Each of these chemical reactions can also be reversed at a high enough temperature. But then energy has to be put in, in order to make the reaction go backwards. For example, when hydrogen combines with oxygen to form water vapor, energy is released. At a high temperature, water vapor can be split into hydrogen and oxygen again. But energy has to be supplied to carry out the splitting. Experiment shows that when a fixed amount of water vapor is split, it uses up as much energy as was released when the water vapor was formed by burning hydrogen in the first place.

Electrical Energy and Heat

At night, when the glowing sun is hidden from us, we get our light from the hot filament of an electric-light bulb. The filament is a metal thread that has been made hot enough to glow. If the hot filament were in contact

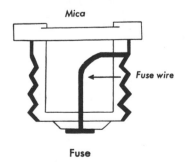

Mica

Fuse wire

Fuse

with air, it would begin to burn. To prevent it from burning, it is sealed into a glass bulb from which the air has been removed.

The electric lamp is another example of energy changing its form: in the lamp electrical energy is changed into heat that flows from the lamp by conduction and as radiated light. The energy that makes the filament glow is produced by an electric current that flows through it. Every electric current produces heat. The larger the current the more heat it produces. An electric wire carrying a very large current may even produce enough heat to start a fire. To protect our homes against fires that may start in this way, we place *fuses* in our electrical circuits. The fuse contains a strip of metal that melts easily. If we turn on too many electrical appliances so that the current becomes too big, the metal strip melts and breaks the circuit. The current stops flowing, the wires remain cool, and a fire is averted.

Trying to Understand Heat

Important studies of heat were made in the eighteenth century by the British scientist Joseph Black. To try to explain the known facts about heat, he proposed the theory that heat is a fluid made up of weightless particles that were so fine they could flow in and out of solid bodies without any trouble.

This theory was not successful, however, because it failed to explain the fact that you could raise the temperature of a body without letting heat flow into it, by rubbing it, for example. It has been replaced by a more successful theory known as the *molecular theory of heat*.

In this theory, each body is pictured as being made of molecules; molecules are seen as made of atoms; and atoms in turn are made of smaller particles including electrons and protons that exert electrical forces on each other. In the remainder of this chapter, we describe some of the details of this theory and show how it explains the principal known facts about heat.

Jumping Molecules

According to the molecular theory, every body is made up of very small particles called *molecules*. A molecule of water is so small that forty million of them, placed side by side, would make a line that is only one inch long. In the air we breathe, there are 443 million million million molecules in a cubic inch. In a solid, the molecules spin and vibrate without moving very far. In a liquid and a gas, they also wander about, darting this way and that through the spaces that separate them, and colliding with each other as well. In the air, at sea level, the molecules are so crowded that each molecule has about fifty billion collisions a second. In a metal there are also free electrons wandering about among the molecules, joining in the constant motion and commotion.

When we look at the objects around us, it seems strange to think that the molecules in them are moving all the time. Unless we stir the water in a glass, it seems so calm and peaceful. But actually there is great agitation beneath this apparent calm. We can see this agitation with the help of a microscope. If you sprinkle a fine powder into water and then look at a drop of the water under a microscope, you see the particles of powder engaged in a wild dance known as *Brownian movement*. They wiggle and jump all the time. This is because the molecules of water keep colliding with them, and push them from side to side. In fact, the warmer the water is, the harder the powder particles seem to be pushed, because they move faster and take bigger jumps. The moving molecules (and free electrons in a metal) all have energy of motion known as *kinetic energy*. The total amount of this kinetic energy of the molecules and free electrons in a body is called the *thermal energy* in the body. The motion of the molecules and free electrons is also related to the temperature of a body. In the molecular theory of heat, temperature is the average energy of the motion of the molecules and free electrons. When a body grows hotter it means that its molecules and free electrons are moving about faster.

The Why and the How

The molecular theory of heat gives us a simple explanation of why and how heat behaves the way it does. Here is the way it explains some of the facts described in Chapter I:

Why heat flows by conduction when a warm body touches a colder body: The molecules in the warm body are moving more vigorously than the molecules in the cool body. Where they are in contact with the less energetic molecules, they push and shove them and make them move faster. Each group of molecules as it gets pushed around begins to stir up its neighbors, too. The commotion spreads into the cooler body, and as its molecules move faster, it becomes warmer. But while the collisions speed up the slower molecules, they slow up the faster ones. As a result, while the cool body grows warmer the warm body grows cooler, until both bodies reach the same temperature.

Why a solid expands when it grows warmer: In a solid, the molecules are attracted to each other by electrical forces. Each molecule is held in place by these forces, so it is not free to wander. But while it stays in place, it can still spin and vibrate. When the solid becomes warmer, the molecules vibrate more vigorously, taking wider swings. Because of these wider swings, the solid fills a larger space.

Why a solid melts when it is heated: When a solid is heated, its molecules vibrate more and more. After a while, they vibrate so hard that they break away from the electrical pull of their neighbors. When this happens, they are free to wander, and the molecules can glide past each other. The solid, which kept its shape, has become a liquid that can flow.

In a liquid, the molecules are not held in place, but they still pull on each other enough to stay close to each other. When the liquid becomes warmer, the molecules move faster and faster, and pull farther apart. Finally, they are so far from each other that the electrical pulls are too weak to bother them at all. Then, except for collisions, each molecule moves as though its neighbors weren't there. When this happens, the liquid evaporates and becomes a gas.

Why heating a gas raises its pressure: The molecules of a gas are moving about at high speed. Even in cold winter air, the average speed of the molecules is over 1400 feet per second. When gas is enclosed in a container, the moving molecules keep hitting against the wall of the container. This steady pushing of the molecules against each square inch of the wall is the pressure of the gas. It is also exerted against any object which is placed inside the gas. If the gas becomes warmer, the molecules move faster. Then they strike the wall of the container harder and more often. That is why the pressure of a gas increases as its temperature goes up.

Why an electric current makes things hot: An electric current in a wire is a stream of electrons being pushed through the wire. The electrons collide with any molecules and free electrons that stand in their way. These collisions cause a great commotion, making the molecules vibrate and the free electrons jump about, and the wire becomes warm. The greater the current is, the more collisions there are, causing greater commotion and a higher temperature.

"Falling" Electrons

To find the explanation for heat flow by radiation we have to look first at what modern theory says about what is inside an atom.

A ball that is resting on the ground is being pulled toward the center of the earth by the force of gravity. We call this pull the weight of the ball. In order to lift the ball above the ground, we have to oppose the force of gravity. We use up energy as we do so. This used-up energy is then stored in the position of the ball. If the ball is released and falls to the ground, the stored-up energy

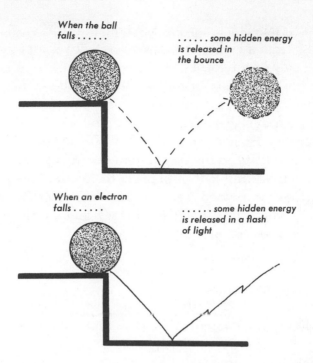

When the ball falls . . . . . .

. . . . . . some hidden energy is released in the bounce

When an electron falls . . . . . .

. . . . . . some hidden energy is released in a flash of light

comes out of its hiding place and appears as the bounce of the ball. Any object that is near the ground has hidden energy in it because of the pull of gravity. The amount of this energy depends on the level at which the body lies. When the body falls from a higher to a lower level, it releases some of this hidden energy.

There is a similar system of forces and energy levels inside the small particles we call atoms. An atom consists of a nucleus surrounded by some electrons. Just as the earth pulls on surrounding objects with the force of gravity, the nucleus pulls on the surrounding electrons with an electrical force. Work has to be done to move an electron from a low level, near the nucleus, to a higher level farther away from the nucleus. At each level, an electron has a certain amount of energy stored in it. If an electron "falls" from a higher to a lower level, it releases some of its energy in the form of a flash of light.

With this picture of energy levels in the atom before us, we can understand why bodies that are made very hot begin to give out light. When the body is heated, its molecules are made to move about faster and faster. At high temperatures the commotion becomes great enough to knock electrons out of place in the atoms. Some of the electrons are pushed up to higher energy levels. When they fall back to a lower level, they give up their extra energy in flashes of light.

"Falling" Molecules

The electrical forces in an atom that hold the electrons near the nucleus reach outside the atom, too. As a result, atoms and molecules pull on their close neighbors. In solids, the pull of these electrical forces serves to keep the atoms and molecules in place. But, just as the electrons may vibrate at different energy levels inside an atom, the atoms and molecules may vibrate at different energy levels in their position with respect to each other. As a result, a molecule, too, may "fall" from a higher energy level to a lower one. When it does, it releases energy in the form of an invisible heat ray called an *infra-red* ray. Infra-red rays, like light rays, are *electromagnetic radiations*. They are electrical and magnetic vibrations that travel through space in the form of waves. Infra-red rays and light rays of various colors differ from each other only in the lengths of their waves. Waves of violet light are so small that there are about 60,000 of them to an inch. Waves of red light are twice as long, so there are about 30,000 of them to an inch. The waves of infra-red rays are longer than the waves of red light.

In any body that contains thermal energy there are vibrating molecules. Among these vibrating molecules there are always some that fall from a higher to a lower energy level. Because of this fact, a hot body is always sending out infra-red rays into space. This is true of the sun, whose rays include infra-red rays as well as light rays. It is true of the hot steam pipes we call "radiators" that warm our rooms in the wintertime. It is also true of the warm bodies of animals. An unheated barn is warm in the wintertime if there are cows in it. Each cow is a radiator sending out infra-red rays in all directions.

Cracked Molecules and Stripped Atoms

If a solid is made hot enough, it melts and becomes a liquid. If a liquid is made hot enough, it evaporates and becomes a gas. In a gas, the atoms and molecules dash about and vibrate at high speed. A molecule consists of a group of atoms held together by electrical forces. If the gas is hot enough, the molecules vibrate so vigorously and collide with such violence that all molecules are cracked open, and their atoms are separated. This happens when the temperature reaches about 4000 degrees Celsius. Above 4000 degrees Celsius no chemical compounds can exist, so no chemical reactions take place. Every atom becomes a lone wolf, whirling and dashing about among its neighbors.

If a gas is heated beyond 4000 degrees Celsius, the collisions begin to crack the atoms. The agitation and the collisions of the atoms tear electrons away from the nuclei. While a complete atom is electrically neutral, a free electron and an atom that has lost electrons carry an electrical charge. These charged particles are known as *ions*. An atom that has lost electrons is said to be *ionized*. At higher and higher temperatures, more and more atoms are stripped of their electrons. At a temperature of 20,000 degrees Celsius, all gases are completely ionized. Their atoms are stripped bare, and the gas consists entirely of naked nuclei and free electrons. A gas that is largely or completely ionized is called a *plasma*. This ionized condition is sometimes referred to as the *fourth state of matter*, distinct from the more common states of solid, liquid, and gas that we meet in everyday experience.

CHAPTER III

Heat Engines

Putting Heat to Work

HEAT CAN BE changed into energy of motion. We
take advantage of this fact in a variety of heat engines
that we use to turn the machinery in our factories, and to
make our automobiles, trucks, planes, and ships run. In
all of these engines we first make a gas very hot, in order
to increase the pressure of the gas. Then the pressure of
the gas supplies the push that makes something move.

Steam Engines

The first practical heat engine that was invented was
the steam engine. In the steam engine, a fire is made in a
furnace, and the heat of the fire is used to boil water to
turn it into steam. The steam flows into one end of a cylinder in which there is a piston attached to a rod. The
pressure of the steam pushes the piston from one end of
the cylinder to the other, and the rod, through a system
of levers, passes this motion on to the machinery that is
being driven by the engine.

In a steam turbine, the steam pressure is put to work in
a different way. It is used to make a *wind of steam* that

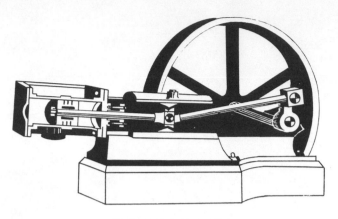

Horizontal steam engine

forces its way through a closed metal shell. Inside the
shell there are several wheels mounted on one axle. The
wheels have vanes, like the vanes of a windmill or a
water wheel. The wind of steam blows against the vanes
as it flows through the shell, and makes the wheels turn.
Before the steam enters the shell, it is heated to a
temperature above 900 degrees Fahrenheit, so that its
pressure becomes about one hundred times as strong as
the pressure of the air. With this high pressure pushing it,
the steam flows through the shell at a speed of 1200 miles
an hour, and makes the wheels in the shell turn at a speed
of 600 miles an hour.

Internal-Combustion Engines

In steam engines, the fire that heats the steam burns in
a separate chamber outside the engine. We have other
engines in which the fire is *inside* the engine itself, so they

are known as *internal-combustion engines.* The gasoline engine of an automobile, the Diesel engine of a large truck, the jet engine of an airplane, and the rocket engine of a spaceship are all examples of internal-combustion engines.

The Gasoline Engine

In a gasoline engine, a mixture of gasoline vapor and air is admitted into one of several cylinders. A piston compresses the mixture by pushing it into a small space at one end of the cylinder. Then an electric spark is allowed to pass through the compressed mixture, setting it on fire in an explosion. The burning mixture produces hot gases at high pressure, and the pressure of these gases pushes the piston back to the other end of the cylinder. In an automobile, the motion of the piston is used to work the levers and gears that make the wheels turn. After the gasoline burns in a cylinder, the burnt gases have to be removed before a fresh mixture of gasoline and air can be

Intake stroke

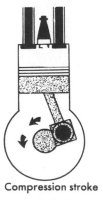
Compression stroke

Power stroke

Exhaust stroke

41

exploded in the cylinder again. The burnt gases are forced out through a valve when the piston returns from the position to which it was pushed by the explosion. In this stage of the motion of the piston, it is pushing the gases instead of being pushed by them, so it is not helping to turn the wheels of the car. Other cylinders in the engine take over the job of turning the wheels until this cylinder is ready for a new explosion.

The Diesel Engine

A Diesel engine burns oil instead of gasoline, and the fire in the cylinders is produced without an electric spark. First, air alone is admitted to a cylinder and is compressed. When the air is compressed, it becomes very hot. Then the fuel is sprayed into the cylinder. When the spray strikes the hot compressed air, it begins to burn immediately. The pressure produced in the hot burnt gases pushes the piston in the cylinder, as it does in a gasoline engine.

Jet Engines

In steam engines, gasoline engines, or Diesel engines, hot gases are produced at high pressure in order to push pistons or vanes. Then the motion of the pistons or vanes is used to drive other machinery. In a jet plane, the push of the hot gases is used directly to push the plane forward without the help of pistons or vanes. The jet engine is a large chamber in which fuel is burned to produce hot gases at high pressure. The pressure forces the gases out through a narrow opening in the tail of the plane. The gases pushed out of the plane push back against it and drive it forward. As in the Diesel engine, the fire is started by spraying fuel into hot compressed air. The air enters the engine through the front end of the plane. Then it is caught by the whirling vanes of a compressor that pushes it into the combustion chamber. The burnt gases that push their way out of the combustion chamber pass through a turbine on the way out. The turbine is attached by a shaft to the compressor, so that as the gases push the turbine, the turbine makes the compressor work. In this way the burnt gases help to bring in a fresh supply of air to keep the fire going.

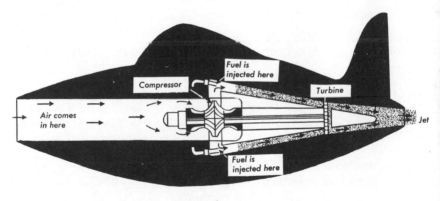

Jet engine

Rocket Engines

A rocket engine works almost like a jet engine, except that it doesn't use air drawn in from the outside. Rockets travel up to high altitudes where there is almost no air, or go to interplanetary space where there is no air at all.

Since they cannot count on getting oxygen from the surrounding air, they take along their own oxygen supply. The oxygen that feeds the fire in a rocket engine is drawn from a tank of liquid oxygen stored in the rocket, or from some chemical compound that has oxygen in it. As in a jet engine, the gases produced by the fire are forced out of a narrow opening and push back against the rocket to make it move.

Scattered Motion

When a swinging hammer smashes down on the head of a nail, it carries energy in the form of energy of motion. The nail moves slightly, and then the energy of motion all disappears. It is converted into thermal energy in both the hammer and the nail, making them warmer. But the thermal energy itself is a kind of energy of motion. In what way does it differ from the energy of motion of the swinging hammer? We have seen part of the answer to this question in the fact that thermal energy is the energy of motion of the molecules. But this is not the whole answer, because the swing of the hammer involves the energy of motion of molecules, too. The hammer is a big collection of molecules, and when the hammer moves, every one of the molecules moves, too. But there is an important difference between the energy of motion the molecules have in this case and the energy that we call thermal energy. In the swinging hammer, all the molecules are moving together down toward the head of the nail. The motion is concentrated and organized. But all this organization disappears when the blow is struck. The molecules that are stirred up by the hammering do not all move together. They vibrate wildly, moving in many different directions at different speeds. The motion is disorderly and scattered. For this reason, the motion involved in thermal energy is often described as *disorderly motion*. When ordinary energy of motion is converted into thermal energy, it means that the motion has become less organized and is spread about in great disorder. The amount of disorder in the motion of a system of bodies can be measured. Scientists call it the *entropy* of the system. When a hammer strikes a nail, organized motion disappears and disordered motion takes its place. So, in the system that includes the hammer and the nail, the entropy, or the amount of disorder, increases.

The Laws of Thermodynamics

When a hammer strikes a nail, energy of motion is changed into thermal energy. In an automobile engine, thermal energy is changed into energy of motion. There is a special branch of physics that studies such interchanges between thermal energy and energy of motion. It is called *thermodynamics*. (*Thermo* means heat, and *dynamics* means motion.) The foundation of this science consists of two facts that stand out from our many experiences with heat and motion. The first of these facts is that heat is a form of energy which can be interchanged with other forms of energy. When such an interchange takes place, the form of the energy changes but the amount does not. When a hammer strikes a nail, some energy of motion disappears but an equal amount of thermal energy appears to take its place. When the hot gases in a cylinder of an automobile engine push the piston up, the gases become cooler in the process. Some thermal energy is lost. But an equal amount of energy of motion (in the motion of the piston) appears to take its place. This fact is usually expressed in the rule that, while energy may change its form, it cannot be created or destroyed. This rule is called the *law of the conservation of energy*. It is also known as the *first law* of thermodynamics.

The second fact, based on long experience with heat engines, is that heat flows naturally from a high temperature, to a lower temperature, but never the other way. We can "pump" heat from a cool body to a warmer body, but the heat won't flow in that direction of its own accord. This fact is usually expressed in the rule that in a system that is sealed off from the rest of the world, it is impossible for heat to flow from a low temperature to a higher temperature *unless some other change takes place at the same time.* Another way of expressing the same rule is to say that the energy in a system tends to become more disordered as time passes, so that its entropy increases. This rule is called the *second law* of thermodynamics.

The Efficiency of a Heat Engine

In a steam engine, energy in the form of heat is used to make hot steam. Then the hot steam is used to push a piston. The outcome of the action of the engine is that some of the thermal energy is withdrawn from the steam and changed into energy of motion. When some thermal energy is withdrawn from the steam, the steam becomes cooler, so its temperature falls to a lower level. But even at this low level, the steam still has plenty of thermal energy in it. While the thermal energy "falls" from a high temperature to a lower temperature, only part of the energy originally put into the steam as heat is withdrawn to be changed into energy of motion. The fraction of the heat input that is actually changed into energy of motion is called the *efficiency* of the engine.

During the nineteenth century when heat engines were being used widely for the first time, engineers were searching for ways of making engines more and more efficient. They did this chiefly by plugging up energy leaks. They used insulating materials to keep the engine from losing too much heat to the surrounding air. They used lubricants to reduce the friction of moving parts, which wasted part of the energy of motion by turning it back again into heat. But all these devices couldn't eliminate energy leaks. They could only reduce them. Then they turned their search for greater efficiency in another direction. They said, suppose we had a perfect heat engine, with no energy leaks at all. Even then, it would not be perfectly efficient, because only some of the heat input is withdrawn to be turned into energy of motion. But maybe if we try out different vapors as carriers of thermal energy, we may find one which converts a greater part of the heat input into energy of motion as the temperature drops between fixed levels. This question was considered by the French engineer and physicist Sadi Carnot, and he came to an unexpected conclusion: the search for a more efficient perfect heat engine was hopeless. He proved that, because of the second law of thermodynamics, any two perfect heat engines that operate between the same temperature levels must have the same efficiency. The efficiency of a perfect heat engine depends on the temperatures at which it operates, but does not depend on the materials of which the engine is made.

Carnot proved his conclusion by a simple chain of arguments. He observed first that the typical heat engine can be made reversible. Working one way, for example, steam expanding in a cylinder pushes a piston. The steam grows cool while some of its thermal energy is turned into energy of motion. But the process can be reversed by merely pushing the piston back. Then the steam is compressed and made warmer, because the energy of motion of the piston is changed into thermal energy. Now suppose, Carnot reasoned, we had two perfect, reversible heat engines that worked between the same temperature levels. Suppose, further, that one of them was more efficient than the other. We could couple the two engines to work together in opposite directions. We could use the less efficient engine to change thermal energy into energy of motion as the thermal energy "fell" from a high temperature to a lower one. We could use the more efficient one to convert the energy of motion back into thermal energy, pumping it from the lower temperature to the higher one. Because of its greater efficiency, the second engine would push thermal energy up to the higher temperature level faster than it was falling through the operation of the first engine. The combined effect of the two engines working together would be to move heat from a lower temperature to a higher temperature without making any other change in the system. But the second law of thermodynamics says that this is impossible. Therefore, one engine cannot be more efficient than another that operates between the same temperatures.

Too Many Temperatures

If you want to take the temperature of a sample of water, you can do it in many different ways. One way, for example, would be to use a mercury thermometer. But you might use an alcohol thermometer instead. On both of these thermometers the reading would be 0 degrees Celsius at the temperature at which water freezes, and 100 degrees Celsius at the temperature at which water boils. So at these temperatures, the two thermometers would agree. But in between these temperatures they need not agree at all. On the mercury thermometer the scale is based on how fast mercury expands as it grows warmer. On the alcohol thermometer it is based on how fast alcohol expands. But the expansion of the two fluids isn't always in step. While the mercury expands halfway up the column from 0 to 100 to give a reading of 50 degrees, the alcohol reaches a different level to give a different reading. The temperature reading on a thermometer depends not only on the level of warmth that it is measuring. It depends also on the material of which the thermometer is made. This, of course, is an inconvenience. It makes it necessary, when we talk about the temperature of a body, to specify which temperature we mean, because a 50 degree temperature as measured by a mercury thermometer is not the same as a 50 degree temperature as measured by an alcohol thermometer. Because of this fact, "temperature" has as many different meanings as there are different kinds of thermometers.

49

The Absolute Scale

Behind the different temperature readings that we get from different thermometers, there is still only one definite level of warmth that they are supposed to measure. Isn't there some way of measuring it that does not depend on the material of which the thermometer is made? The British scientist Lord Kelvin showed that there is, if we take advantage of Carnot's discovery about the efficiency of perfect, reversible heat engines. The efficiency of such an engine depends on the levels of warmth between which it operates, but not on the materials of which it is made. So an absolute temperature scale, independent of our choice of thermometer, can be constructed from the study of the efficiency of these engines. In the scale introduced by Lord Kelvin, he fixed the number that represents any level of warmth by introducing two rules: 1) when heat falls in a perfect heat engine from a high temperature to a lower temperature, the ratio of the drop in temperature to the high temperature from which it falls should be the efficiency of the engine; 2) the size of a degree is chosen so that, as in the Celsius scale, there are 100 degrees between the freezing point and boiling point of water. The absolute scale, based on these rules, is now known as the Kelvin scale. On this scale, the number 0 represents the temperature of a body when *all* the thermal energy in it has been withdrawn. Since thermal energy is the disordered motion of molecules, this means that absolute zero is the temperature at which the molecules would not move at all. Absolute zero can be approached, but it can never actually be reached.

On the Kelvin scale, the freezing point of water is about 273 degrees. So, to change a temperature reading from the Celsius scale to the Kelvin scale, simply add the number 273. How different temperature levels are represented in the Fahrenheit, Celsius, and Kelvin scales is shown in the table below.

| TEMPERATURE LEVEL | FAHRENHEIT | NUMBER OF DEGREES | |
		CELSIUS	KELVIN
Absolute Zero	−459.6	−273.1	0
Boiling point of helium	−452	−268.9	4.2
Boiling point of hydrogen	−423	−252.7	20.4
Boiling point of oxygen	−297	−183	90
Freezing point of water	32	0	273
Boiling point of water	212	100	373
Boiling point of sulfur	833	445	718
Boiling point of silver	1760	960	1233
Boiling point of gold	1945	1063	1336
Melting point of iron	2795	1539	1812
Flame of oxyaluminum torch	6332	3500	3773
Surface of the sun	10,340	5727	6000

CHAPTER IV

Ways of Measuring Temperature

How the Thermometer Grew Up

THE MERCURY thermometer that we use to measure the temperature of the air in our homes looks like a very simple instrument. It is not so simple, though. It is the product of many inventions, introduced gradually during a period of more than a hundred years. The first step toward developing the thermometer as we know it was taken by the Italian scientist Galileo some time between 1592 and 1597. Galileo knew that fluids expand when they grow warmer, and he recognized that this expansion could be used to measure changes in temperature. The fluid he chose to use in the first thermometer was air. He warmed the air in a glass flask with a long neck, causing the air to expand so that some of it flowed out of the flask. Then he mounted the flask upside down over a jar of water, with the neck of the flask under the water. When the air in the flask cooled, the water, pushed by the pressure of the atmosphere, rose part way up the neck of the flask. After that, the height of the water in the neck of the flask served as a rough indicator of temperature, because when the air in the flask grew warmer, it expanded and pushed the water column down. When the air in the flask became colder, it contracted and the water column climbed to a higher level.

Galileo's thermometer could give only rough measures of temperature, because its operation depends on the pressure of the atmosphere, something that Galileo himself did not understand. We know today that the height to which the water column rises in his thermometer is the result of a battle of pressures. The pressure of the atmosphere tries to push the water column up. When the water rises, it compresses the air in the flask. The compressed air in the flask acts like a spring, and its own pressure pushes back against the water column, trying to force it down again. The water settles at that level where the combined push of the pressure of the air in the flask and the weight of the water that rises out of the jar are just enough to balance the pressure of the atmosphere. But the pressure of the atmosphere changes from time to time. So the height of the water column may change even

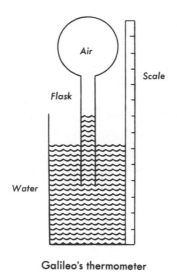

Galileo's thermometer

when the temperature remains fixed. Galileo's thermometer really records the *combined results* of changes in temperature and atmospheric pressure, and not changes in temperature alone.

A scale mounted next to the neck of the flask helped to show how the height of the water column changed from hour to hour. More meaning was given to this scale when the Italian professor Sanctorius introduced two fixed reference points on it. He marked on the scale a cold point, the level to which water rose when the flask was cooled by snow, and a warm point, the level to which it rose when it was warmed by a candle flame.

The thermometer began to look more like the one we know today when the French physician Jean Rey decided in 1630 to use the expansion of a liquid rather than the expansion of air to measure changes in temperature. In Rey's thermometer, water rose from a bulb into a glass tube, rising higher when the water expanded, and dropping when the water contracted. The tube was open at the top, so the water in the tube slowly evaporated. The loss of water made the reading on Rey's thermometer inaccurate. To prevent evaporation, it was necessary to seal the liquid into the tube. This improvement was introduced around 1650 by Ferdinand II, Grand Duke of Tuscany, who made the first alcohol thermometer in a sealed tube. In 1694, Renaldini introduced the fixed reference points we use today, the freezing point and the boiling point of water. In 1717, Fahrenheit began making accurate alcohol and mercury thermometers with the scale that calls the freezing point 32 degrees and the boiling point 212 degrees. The centigrade scale, from which the Celsius scale was derived, was first used in 1710 by the Swedish scientist Elvius.

The common mercury thermometer can work only as long as the mercury in it is liquid and the glass that contains the mercury is solid. Mercury freezes at 38 degrees below zero, Fahrenheit, so a mercury thermometer cannot be used below this temperature. Glass begins to get soft at about 650 degrees Fahrenheit, so the mercury in a glass thermometer cannot be used above this temperature. Beyond these two levels other ways of measuring temperature have to be used.

The Gas Pressure Thermometer

When gas in a closed container is warmed up, two results are possible. The gas may expand, if it is allowed to, as it was in Galileo's thermometer. Or, if it is confined to a fixed space, its pressure will change. In that case, the

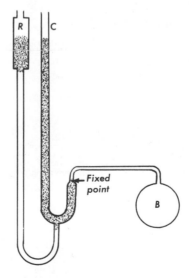

Constant volume gas thermometer

change in pressure serves as a measure of the change in temperature. This principle is used in the constant volume gas thermometer. The way in which the gas thermometer works is shown in the diagram on page 55. The gas is enclosed in the bulb marked B. A thin tube joins the bulb to the mercury-filled U-shaped tube marked C. This tube is joined to the mercury reservoir marked R. On the right-hand arm of the U-shaped tube, a fixed point is marked. By raising or lowering the mercury reservoir, the top of the mercury in the tube can be brought to this fixed point. In this way, the volume of the gas in the bulb is kept constant. The pressure of the gas in the bulb is balanced by the pressure of the mercury column in the left arm of the U-shaped tube and of the atmosphere above it. So the height of the mercury column plus the pressure of the atmosphere serves as a measure of the pressure of the gas in the bulb. This in turn serves as a measure of its temperature.

The gases commonly used in a constant volume gas thermometer are hydrogen, helium, nitrogen, or air. A nitrogen thermometer is used for temperatures up to about 1550 degrees Celsius. Hydrogen or helium are used for temperature measurements below zero degrees Celsius.

The Vapor Pressure Thermometer

A different kind of gas thermometer makes use of the fact that a liquid tends to evaporate, even when its temperature is below the boiling point. Suppose, for example, some liquid oxygen is placed in a closed container, with a vacuum above it. The molecules of the

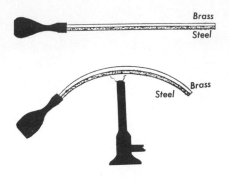

liquid air are constantly jumping around. Some of the
molecules at the surface of the liquid jump right out of
the liquid into the space above it, so the space is soon
filled with some oxygen vapor or gas. As more and more
molecules jump out of the liquid, the pressure of the
vapor increases until the number of molecules jumping
out of the liquid is balanced by the number jumping back
from the vapor. The pressure that is finally reached in
the vapor depends on the temperature of the liquid, so it
serves as a measure of this temperature. Vapor pressure
thermometers, using liquid oxygen or hydrogen, are used
for making measurements at very low temperatures in
the laboratory.

The Bimetal Thermometer

Solids, as well as fluids, expand when they are heated.
So it is possible to use the expansion of a solid for measuring temperature. This is usually done by using two metals
that expand at different rates. A long strip is cut from
each metal, and the two are joined to each other back to

57.

back to make a single piece of bimetal. When the temperature rises, both metals grow longer, but one actually stretches more than the other. As a result, the double strip of metal curls. The curling and uncurling of the metal strip can be used to turn a pointer which indicates the temperature on a dial. This is the way the ordinary oven thermometer works.

The Resistance Thermometer

We can start an electric current flowing through a wire by placing a voltage, or electrical pressure, across it. How much current will flow through the wire depends on the *resistance* of the wire. The wire is like an obstacle course through which electrons are trying to pass. A wire with a high resistance places many obstacles in the electrons' path. A wire with a low resistance permits them to flow more freely. In 1887, H.L. Callenda found that the resistance of a wire is not fixed, but changes with its temperature. This fact makes it possible to use a wire with an electric current in it as a thermometer. The wire that is usually used for this purpose is a thread of platinum, about six feet long and about one-hundredth of an inch thick, wound on a coil. When the temperature in the coil rises, its resistance rises and the current flowing through it drops. The strength of the current is measured by means of electric meters, and the temperature is calculated from this measurement. The platinum resistance thermometer is used for both high and low temperature measurements. It will measure temperatures as high as 1200 degrees Celsius or as low as –259 degrees Celsius, only fourteen degrees above absolute zero.

The Thermocouple

We saw in Chapter I that an electric current flowing through a wire produces heat. In 1821, Thomas Seebeck discovered that the process can be reversed in an electric circuit that uses two kinds of wire, each made of a different metal. In such a circuit, called a *thermocouple*, heat can be turned into electrical energy. The two metals are joined to each other at two places in the circuit. If one junction is made warmer than the other, an electrical voltage is created between the junctions, and an electric current begins to flow around the circuit. The greater the temperature difference between the junctions, the higher the voltage that is created. This fact makes it possible to use a thermocouple to measure temperatures. The simplified diagram below shows how a thermocouple might be used to measure the temperature of a candle flame.

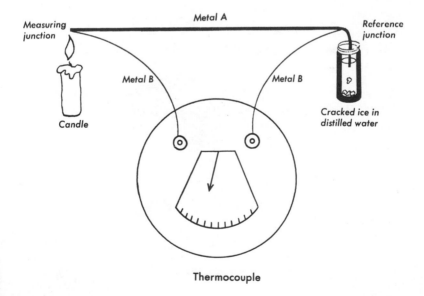

Thermocouple

The two metals in the thermocouple are referred to as metals A and B. One junction is exposed to the heat of the candle flame until it becomes as warm as the flame. The other junction is kept at a temperature of 0 degrees Celsius by dipping it into a Thermos bottle filled with cracked ice in distilled water. The electric meter measures the voltage that is produced, and the temperature of the flame is calculated from the voltage.

The metals used in a thermocouple may be pure metals like platinum, iron, or copper, or they may be alloys (mixtures of metals). The alloys used most often are *chromel*, a mixture of nickel and chromium, *alumel*, a mixture of nickel, aluminum, silicon and manganese, *constantan*, a mixture of copper and nickel, and *platinum-rhodium*, a mixture of platinum and rhodium. A thermocouple in which platinum is joined to platinum-rhodium

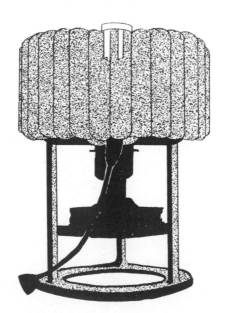

can measure temperatures from 0 degrees to 1450 degrees Celsius. For low temperatures, from –200 degrees to 0 degrees Celsius, a thermocouple of copper joined to constantan is used. A chromel to alumel couple can measure from –200 to 1200 degrees Celsius. An iron to constantan couple can measure from –200 to 750 degrees Celsius.

When metals are used in a thermocouple, the voltage produced in it is very small. A temperature difference of 100 degrees Celsius produces from one to seven thousandths of a volt. Recently it was found that more than ten times as much voltage can be produced if certain minerals called *semiconductors* are used instead of metal. This improvement in thermocouples makes it possible to use them as a new kind of battery, in which heat is changed directly into electrical energy. The drawing on page 60 shows a "battery" in which the heat of a kerosene lamp produces enough electrical power to operate a radio.

Measuring Temperature at a Distance

In industry it is sometimes necessary to measure the temperature inside a furnace. The furnace may be so hot that it is not practical to try to put any kind of thermometer into it. It is still possible to measure the temperature though, even while standing at a distance from the furnace, because the furnace sends out heat rays, and these can be caught and measured. An instrument that measures temperatures from the heat rays it receives is called a *pyrometer*.

Every body whose temperature is above absolute zero sends out radiation, which travels away from the body in

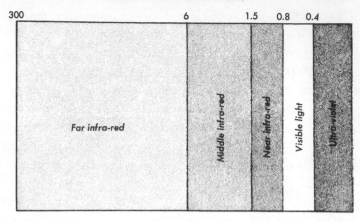

WAVE LENGTHS IN MICRONS

| 300 | 6 | 1.5 | 0.8 | 0.4 |

Far infra-red

Middle infra-red

Near infra-red

Visible light

Ultra-violet

Wave lengths of radiation

the form of waves. The radiation sent out by a body is a mixture of rays of many different wave lengths. The wave lengths are all very small, so it is convenient to express them in terms of a tiny unit of length known as a *micron*. A micron is one-millionth of a meter, while a meter is about 39 inches long. There are 25,400 microns in an inch. The wave lengths of the rays sent out by bodies because of their heat may be as high as 300 microns or as short as .3 micron. This range of radiation includes three kinds of rays. The shortest waves are those of *ultra-violet rays*. These are the invisible rays in sunlight that cause sunburn. Slightly longer are the rays of *visible light*, which range from .4 micron to .8 micron in length. The longest waves, ranging from .8 micron to 300 microns, are also invisible and are known as *infra-red rays*. Most of the rays that warm bodies send out are infrared, so pyrometers are designed to catch, detect, and measure infra-red radiation.

Although the radiation from a body is a mixture of many wave lengths, it is possible to separate the different wave lengths from each other by means of filters, and then measure the amount of energy in each of the wave lengths. The results of these measurements can be recorded in a graph, in which each wave length is shown as a point on a horizontal line, and the energy in that wave length is shown as the height of the graph above that point. Experiment and theory show that the position, the height, and the shape of the graph depend on the temperature of the body which is sending out the rays. Typical graphs for temperatures ranging from 20 degrees Celsius to 920 degrees Celsius are shown below.

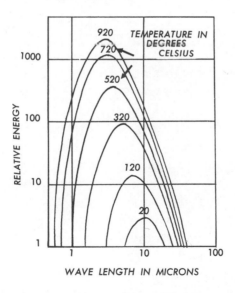

WAVE LENGTH IN MICRONS

A look at these graphs shows that there are three different ways in which the radiation sent out by a warm body depends on its temperature. Notice, first, that the hotter a body is, the more energy it radiates. So one way of measuring the temperature of a body is to measure the total radiation in all wave lengths that it sends out.

Notice, secondly, that the curve for each temperature has a highest point, showing a wave length in which more energy is concentrated than in any other wave length. This concentration wave length is different for each temperature. So another way of measuring temperature is to identify the wave length that carries the largest share of the energy that the body radiates. Notice, thirdly, that each graph has a special position and shape that distinguishes it from its neighbors. A third way of measuring the temperature of a warm body is to plot the graph showing the energy in all the wave lengths it radiates, and then see which one of a standard set of graphs it fits most closely.

A typical pyrometer measures the energy in the rays it receives by converting it into an electrical signal. First the rays pass through a filter to screen out some of them, so that only particular wave lengths remain to be measured. Then lenses and mirrors focus these rays on a detector unit. If the detector is a thermocouple, the focused rays warm up one of its junctions and start an electric current flowing through it. The detector may also be a conductor through which an electric current is already flowing. When the rays fall on the conductor, its resistance changes. Then the current changes, too, and the change is a clue to the amount of energy in the rays that were received.

There is one type of pyrometer in which the *visible light* sent out by a very hot body is used to measure its temperature. This is done by comparing it with the light of a lamp filament. The lamp filament is viewed through a telescope against the light of the hot body as a background. The temperature and brightness of the filament are varied by changing the amount of current flowing through it. When the filament is very hot, it looks brighter than the background. When the filament is cool, it looks darker than the background. At an intermediate temperature, it has the same brightness as the hot body and disappears against the background. The current at which the filament disappears from view is the clue to the temperature of the radiating body. A disappearing filament pyrometer was used to measure the temperature of the lava erupted from the Kilauea volcano in Hawaii.

The Temperature of a Star

The same methods that are used for measuring the temperature of a furnace a few feet away can be used to measure the surface temperature of a star millions of miles away. All we have to do is catch some of the rays of starlight that reach the earth and see which wave lengths carry the most energy. The starlight is caught in a telescope and allowed to pass through filters, so that the energy in particular wave lengths can be measured separately. The lens or mirror of the telescope brings the light to a focus on a sensitive thermocouple which converts some of the heat energy received into an electrical signal. The energy graph that is plotted for the star is then fitted against the standard graphs described on page 63. The temperature obtained in this way is called the *color temperature* of the star. For a bluish-white star the surface temperature may be as high as 80,000 degrees Celsius. A red star is cool by comparison, with a temperature of only 2600 degrees.

An instrument sometimes used for measuring small amounts of radiation is a special kind of *radiometer*, made of lightweight vanes hung inside a vacuum tube. When rays strike the vanes of the radiometer, they make it turn the way water turns a water wheel. In 1928, C. G. Abbot, of the Smithsonian Institution in Washington, D.C., made a radiometer to measure the energy in the rays of the brighter stars. He needed vanes that would be delicate enough to be pushed by starlight, so he made them out of the wings of a housefly. Each vane was made of a triple layer of wings, and the front layer was blackened with lampblack paint to make it absorb all the starlight that would strike it. The vanes were hung in a quartz tube at the end of a thin quartz fiber about 6 inches long. The strength of rays striking the vanes was measured by the amount of twisting they caused in the fiber when the vanes turned.

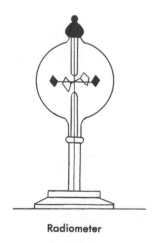

Radiometer

The moon and the planets do not shine with their own light the way the sun and the stars do. They merely reflect light from the sun. But, because they have temperatures above absolute zero, these bodies do radiate their own invisible infra-red rays. So it is possible to measure their temperatures, too, by catching and measuring this infra-red radiation. The temperature of Mercury, the planet closest to the sun, is found to be about 330 degrees Celsius. Venus has a temperature of 470 degrees Celsius. The temperature on Mars varies from –120 degrees to –27 degrees. Jupiter is as cold as –135 degrees. Saturn reaches –170 degrees and Uranus is below –185 degrees. The moon, while it is as cold as Saturn when it faces away from the sun, gets as hot as boiling water when it is flooded with bright sunlight.

Empty Space and the Centers of Stars

In between the stars there is empty space. Actually, this space is not completely empty. There are scattered dust particles in this space. These particles are warmed slightly by the light they receive from the surrounding stars. Then, because they have temperatures above absolute zero, the dust particles send out infra-red rays of their own. By turning our telescopes toward dark parts of the sky we can measure this radiation of the dust particles, and then compare it with the amount of starlight we figure that the particles receive. From this comparison it is possible to calculate what the temperature of the dust particles is. The average temperature of interstellar dust turns out to be about three degrees above absolute zero on the Kelvin scale. This is the lowest temperature found in nature, but not the lowest temperature ever measured. Scientists can produce lower temperatures in their laboratories, as we shall see in Chapter VI.

The rays we receive from a star are a direct clue to its surface temperature. They also give us an indirect clue to the temperature at the center of the star. Astronomers have discovered formulas which relate the brightness of a star to its mass, or how heavy it is. In cases where they can also measure the size of the star, they then know whether this mass is condensed in a small space or spread out thin in a big space. From this information they can calculate the temperature *inside* the star. The temperature at the center of the sun is calculated to be about 20 million degrees Celsius. The temperature inside Sirius, the star that appears brightest in the sky, is about 25 million degrees Celsius. In some dwarf stars, which are only one-fourth as wide as the sun, but very much heavier than the sun, the temperature is about 50 million degrees Celsius.

Taking Pictures in the Dark

The ordinary camera takes pictures with the help of light. Light is reflected from the object being photographed. Some of this light is caught by the lens of the camera and then focused on a photographic film. The light causes a chemical change in the film. Then, when the film is developed, a dark spot appears wherever light had fallen on it. The pattern of light and dark spots is the negative picture on the film. When a print is made from a negative, the pattern is reversed. Each dark spot on the negative produces a light spot on the print, and each light spot on the negative produces a dark spot on the print. Then the printed picture is an image of the object that was photographed.

Because light is needed to "expose" the film in a camera, it used to be taken for granted that you cannot take pictures in the dark. This is no longer true. The development of radiometers and pyrometers that are sensitive to infra-red heat rays has made it possible to take pictures in *total darkness*. The picture below, showing a man riding on a motorcycle, was taken in the dark by means of the infra-red rays radiating from the man's body. The picture was taken with a Barnes Far Infrared Camera, shown in the photograph on page 70.

Photograph taken with infra-red rays. *Barnes Engineering Company*

You will notice that the picture of the man is made up of a series of horizontal lines, one under the other, and each line is a chain of dark and light spots. This is because the picture is not taken all at once, but is taken a little at a time by "scanning" the man's body. Just as, when you read a book, your eye sweeps across the page, one line at a time, the camera sweeps across the man's body, one line at a time, receiving infra-red rays from different parts of the body in turn. The radiation detector inside the camera receives these rays and converts them into an electrical signal, making the signal strong when the rays are strong, and weak when the rays are weak. The signal is used to control the brightness of a thin beam of light coming from inside the instrument. The beam of light is reflected from a mirror onto a

A far infra-red camera. *Barnes Engineering Company*

photographic film in an ordinary camera, striking the film on a small spot. As the instrument scans the man's body, sweeping across one line at a time, the mirror moves in step with it, making the light beam sweep across the film, one line at a time. Meanwhile, the electrical signal is making the light stronger or weaker, in step with the strength of the infra-red rays received from the man's body. So the image produced on the film matches the warm and cool spots on the man's face, hands, and clothing. With a camera like this, an airplane flying over a city at night could photograph the city during a complete blackout. While all lights are out, each building would reveal itself by the infra-red rays that come from it.

Taking the Temperature of the Past

A geologist can look at a rock that was formed hundreds of millions of years ago, and tell you what the temperature was in the *magma*, or melted rock, from which the rock was formed. This is because the rock itself has a built-in record of the temperature at which it was born. Laboratory experiments show that when crystals form in a hardening magma, the type of crystal formed depends on the temperature. So, by identifying the crystals that are in the rock, the geologist can tell what the temperature was when the crystal was formed. The temperature at which most mineral veins were formed ranges from 100 degrees Celsius, the temperature of boiling water, to 570 degrees Celsius.

There is also a record in the sea of how warm the water was far back in the past. The record is in the sea shells that lie on the sea floor. The fact that sea shells can serve as a geological thermometer was discovered by the American scientist Harold Urey in 1947. Sea animals form their shells out of chemical compounds called *carbonates*. These compounds contain oxygen that the animal draws out of the surrounding sea water. There are three different kinds of oxygen, called oxygen 16, oxygen 17, and oxygen 18, each having a different weight. They are mixed together in different amounts in carbonates that are formed in water. Urey found that the amount of each type of oxygen found in a carbonate depends on how warm the water was when the carbonate was formed in it. A difference of one degree Celsius in temperature produces a difference of two-hundredths of one per cent in the ratio of oxygen 18 to oxygen 16 in the carbonate. Urey first made theoretical calculations that showed how the ratio varied with temperature. Then he and his students checked the theory by experiment, by actually growing sea shells in water kept at different temperatures.

The sea shells on the sea floor contain a record of the past, because they have been piling up there for millions of years. The oldest shells are at the bottom of the heap. By taking borings from the sea floor, the scientist gets a sample of the shells in each of the many layers that are piled on top of each other. He can judge how long the shell has been lying there by how deeply buried it is and what kind of shell it is. Then he knows some shells were formed 100,000 years ago, others 200,000 years ago, and so on. After he examines the oxygen in these shells, he then knows what the temperature of the sea was that far back in the past. The chart opposite shows the changes in the temperature of the sea during the last 300,000 years, measured from the oxygen content of the different layers of six sea-bottom borings. The four cold dips represent the Ice Ages, when big ice sheets covered large parts of Europe and North America.

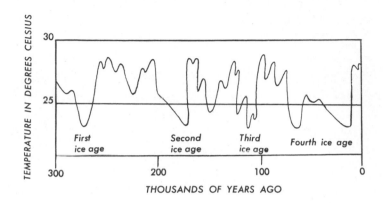

Urey's geological thermometer is so sensitive that it can even trace the temperature changes in the lifetime of a single animal. In 1950 he analyzed the skeleton of an animal that had lived 150 million years ago. The skeleton of this animal is deposited in growth rings. By analyzing the different layers of rings, Urey traced the changes in temperature from year to year, and even from season to season within one year, as the animal grew up. The chemical analysis showed that this particular animal was born in the summertime, lived four years, and died in the spring!

Measuring Temperature with X-rays

When a gas is heated, and is permitted to expand so that its pressure does not change, the hotter the gas becomes, the more it spreads out. The more it spreads out, the less gas there is in any fixed volume. So the gas becomes less and less dense with higher temperature. For this reason, one way of taking the temperature of a gas whose pressure is known is to measure its density. An interesting way in which this is sometimes done is to send X-rays through the gas. Some of the X-rays collide with the molecules of the gas and are absorbed, so they never get through to the other side of the container. The denser the gas is, the more collisions there are, and the more the X-rays are absorbed. Since the absorption depends on the density of the gas, and the density depends on the temperature, the amount of the X-rays that are absorbed serves as a measure of the temperature of the gas.

Measuring Temperature with Sound

Another way of measuring the temperature of a gas is to send some sound through it. Sound travels through the gas at a definite speed, but the speed depends on the temperature. So, if the speed of the sound is measured, the temperature of the gas can be calculated. To make the sound and measure its speed, two sparks are produced by electrical discharges through the gas. The sparks are separated by a measured distance. One of the sparks is the sound maker. The sound of the spark travels through the gas until it reaches the other spark. This second spark is the sound receiver. It is connected to an electrical measuring instrument called an *oscillograph*, which keeps track of changes in the voltage across the spark gap. When the sound reaches the receiver there is a sudden increase in the spark voltage. So the oscillograph record shows *when* the sound reached the second spark. Knowing the distance between the two sparks and the time it took the sound to cross this distance, it is possible to calculate the speed of the sound, and then figure out the temperature of the gas.

CHAPTER V

From Gas Range to Plasma Jet

Making Things Hot

PERHAPS HALF a million years ago, some primitive man found a burning tree in the forest, and instead of running away from it, used a glowing twig to warm himself or cook his supper. This step started mankind on the long road to civilization. As people followed this road, they developed many activities in which they needed high temperatures. They also discovered more and more ways of producing the high temperatures they needed. The oldest of these, making a *fire*, is still one of the most useful. Another old method, concentrating the rays of the sun, has been perfected in the *solar furnace*. But we also have new methods, based on the use of *electricity*, through which we produce the highest temperatures that man has ever made and maintained for a long period of time. By using *atomic explosions* we can reach even higher temperatures than these, but so far they last for only a fraction of a second.

Fast Fires

A fire, as we saw in Chapter I, is a chemical reaction in which other elements combine with oxygen, and energy is released when the reaction takes place. To reach high temperatures in a fire, we try to speed up the rate at which it releases energy. This can be done by using special fuels that release extra-large amounts of energy. But it can also be done by making the fire burn faster.

To understand how a fire can be made to burn faster, let us examine what happens when a lump of coal burns. The coal is a mass of carbon atoms. The carbon atoms burn when they combine with oxygen from the air. But not all of the carbon atoms in the lump are near enough to oxygen atoms to combine with them. The atoms that lie on the surface of the lump are right next to the air. So the oxygen reaches them without any trouble, and they burn. But the atoms that are inside the lump are shielded from the air by the atoms of carbon that surround them. They get no air, and do not burn until the layers of carbon around them have burned away first. A lump of coal burns only on its surface.

New
surfaces

The drawing above shows a typical lump of coal. Alongside this drawing is another showing what the lump would look like if it were broken into two pieces. Notice that when the lump is broken, two new surfaces appear at the break. In the broken pieces, atoms that used to be deep inside the lump are now at the surface, in contact with air. This suggests a way of speeding up the rate at which a solid fuel burns. If the fuel is broken into small pieces, more of its atoms will lie on the surface, exposed to the air. As a result, more of them will burn at the same time, and the fuel will burn up faster. A solid fuel burns fastest when it is ground up into a fine powder.

When we use a gas as a fuel, we don't have to bother about breaking it up into small pieces. It is already made up of the smallest pieces possible, the separate molecules of the gas. Our only problem when we burn gas is to make sure that there is enough oxygen next to the molecules. This is done by mixing the gas with air before it burns. In the gas stove in your kitchen, for example, there is an air hole at the base of each gas burner. As the gas flows from the pipe into the burner, air flows into the hole and mixes with the gas. Then, when the mixture is ignited in the burner, each molecule of fuel has oxygen right next to it with which it can combine.

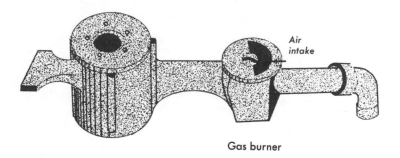

Air intake

Gas burner

When we use a liquid fuel, we break it up into small pieces by turning it into a vapor. Then the scattered molecules in the vapor are easily mixed with air. In an automobile, for example, the liquid gasoline passes through the carburetor before it is fed to the cylinders. The carburetor works like an atomizer, blowing the gasoline into a fine spray and mixing it with air. The gasoline in the spray evaporates quickly, so that the gasoline is in vapor form by the time it gets to the cylinders where it burns.

Breaking up the fuel has the purpose of bringing more fuel to the oxygen. We can also speed up the process of bringing fuel and oxygen together by bringing more oxygen to the fuel. As the fuel burns, it uses up the oxygen that is near it. The burning will continue only if a fresh supply of oxygen is moved in to take the place of the oxygen that has been used up. So a fire has to be supplied with a *draft*, a steady flow of fresh air moving in toward the fire with oxygen, and then moving away from the fire to remove the gases that result from the burning of the fuel. In an ordinary fire, this draft develops automatically when the warmed-up air over the fire rises and cooler air flows in to take its place. In some fires we speed up the draft by using compressed air, and blowing the air in toward the fire under high pressure. The use of compressed air speeds up the flow of oxygen in two ways. First, because it is compressed, any given volume of it contains more air, and therefore more oxygen, than the same volume of ordinary air does. Secondly, it moves faster, since it is being pushed harder, so the extra supply of oxygen moves in extra fast. A plumber's torch and some welding torches use compressed air for their oxygen supply.

The only part of the air that feeds a fire is the oxygen that is in it. But the oxygen is only one-fifth of the air. So four-fifths of the air that flows into a fire doesn't help it burn at all. We get a further increase in the speed with which a fire burns when we supply it with pure oxygen instead of compressed air. The oxygen used for this purpose is stored in liquid form in a tank, and it is allowed to evaporate a little at a time as it is used. (The way in which liquid oxygen is obtained is described in the next chapter.) Welding torches often use pure oxygen.

Another way of bringing oxygen to a fire is to hide it first in an oxygen compound, and then mix the compound with the fuel. The compound chosen to carry the oxygen is one which gives up its oxygen easily, once the fuel starts burning. This method is often used when the fuel is a powdered solid. In gunpowder, for example, the fuel is powdered charcoal and sulfur, and the oxygen is hidden in the potassium nitrate that is mixed with them.

Hot Fires

The flame in an ordinary gas range like the one in your kitchen produces a temperature of about 1700 degrees Celsius. We can make the flame hotter by using a different kind of gas, fed with compressed air. An acetylene torch, for example, produces a flame whose temperature is about 2250 degrees Celsius.

The hottest fires produced at ordinary atmospheric pressure use powdered metals as fuel. In the *thermit* process, used for welding iron, the fuel is powdered aluminum. The aluminum powder is mixed with a kind of iron rust, which is a compound of iron and oxygen. If two pieces of iron are to be welded together, they are put next to each other. The mixture is placed over the joint and is ignited. The rust gives up its oxygen to the aluminum and makes it burn. The burning aluminum produces a temperature of 3000 degrees Celsius. The high temperature melts the iron at the joint, and also melts the iron that was in the rust. The melted iron seals the joint to make one piece of metal out of two.

If aluminum powder is burned with pure oxygen, as it is in the oxyaluminum torch, it produces a temperature of 3500 degrees Celsius. The oxyaluminum flame is hot enough to burn a hole right through a solid block of concrete. A temperature of 4500 degrees can be reached by burning powdered beryllium instead of aluminum. An even hotter flame is produced by some rocket fuels burned at very high pressure. For example, cyanogen combining with fluorine instead of oxygen, at a pressure twenty times as high as the pressure of the atmosphere, produces a temperature of 4700 degrees Celsius.

Using High Temperature

We have many uses for high temperatures. We use them in heat engines, like those described in Chapter III, to produce high pressures that make machinery move. We use them in torches to melt metals. The melting may serve to cut the metal into pieces, or work the opposite way by fusing pieces together. We often melt metals, too, to pour them into molds and give them the shape we want.

One of the chief uses of high temperature is to stir up chemical activity. The steel industry and the nitrate industry give us two important examples. In an open-hearth furnace we use a temperature of 2000 degrees Celsius to promote the chemical change that removes iron from its ore. The way this is done is described in the book *Fire in Your Life.** In the nitrate industry, we use a temperature of 700 degrees Celsius in the Haber process, which makes the nitrogen compound ammonia out of nitrogen taken from the air. This is the first step in a chain of chemical changes by which the nitrogen is built into the compounds that we use as fertilizers or explosives. At a higher temperature, it is possible to start this chain in a different way by a new process that produces nitric oxide instead of ammonia in the first step. In this new process, fuel gas is burned with preheated air to produce a temperature of 2100 degrees Celsius. At this temperature, nitrogen can be combined with oxygen to form nitric oxide. The oxide is cooled quickly to a temperature of 1500 degrees Celsius, and then is combined with water to form nitric acid. The new process may soon replace the Haber process as the chief method used for making nitrogen compounds.

High temperature is an important tool in scientific research. We see an interesting example of this fact in the recent testing of theories of how granite is formed in the earth. There were several theories competing with each other. One theory said that granite is formed when magma, or hot melted rock, cools. To test this melted rock theory, geologists melted a mixture of quartz and albite, two of the minerals found in granite, and then cooled the mixture. They mixed the quartz and albite in many different proportions. If the mixture was two-thirds quartz, it remained a liquid when it was hot until the temperature fell to 740 degrees Celsius. Then the

---

*By the same author. New York: The John Day Company, 1955.

quartz and albite both began to form crystals at the same time. If the mixture was more than two-thirds quartz, as it cooled from a temperature above 740 degrees only quartz crystallized out, until the temperature reached 740 degrees. By that time, the share of the quartz was reduced to two-thirds of the mixture. After that, as the magma cooled more, both minerals crystallized together. If the mixture was less than two-thirds quartz, as it cooled from a temperature above 740 degrees only albite crystallized out, until the temperature reached 740 degrees. By that time, the share of the quartz was raised to two-thirds of the mixture. Then, once again, both minerals crystallized together as the magma cooled some more. In other words, when the minerals crystallize together, they do so in a fixed ratio that could be measured in the laboratory. The ratio turns out to be just that ratio in which they are found together in granite. This fact is strong evidence in favor of the theory that in nature granite is formed from magmas of mixed quartz and albite.

Shock-Wave Heat

The high temperatures described above are temperatures we produce on purpose, because we find them useful. There are also high temperatures we produce unintentionally, and we find them a nuisance. A simple example is the heating produced by the friction of moving parts in a machine. We use lubricants to counteract this heating, because if the machine gets too hot, it will be damaged. An extreme example is the heating produced by the shock wave that is created when a plane or a rocket pushes its way through the air faster than the speed of sound. Just as the hammering of a nail produces heating, the hammering of the air in the shock wave produced heating, too. When the moving body has four times the speed of sound, the temperature in the shock wave it produces is 1000 degrees Celsius. At ten times the speed of sound, the temperature reached is 3000 degrees Celsius. At twenty times the speed of sound, the temperature is 6000 degrees Celsius, about the same as the temperature on the surface of the sun. High-speed rockets are accompanied by a shock wave in which the temperature may reach as high as 38,000 degrees Celsius. How to keep the rocket from being destroyed by such a high temperature is a big problem for the engineers who design rockets.

Shock-wave temperatures can be produced in the laboratory as well as in the air. The apparatus used is a special shock tube consisting of two compartments separated by a diaphragm. A gas is pumped into one of the compartments. As more and more gas is pumped in, the pressure of the gas rises higher and higher. Finally, the pressure is so high that the gas breaks through the diaphragm and surges into the other compartment, traveling faster than sound. This sudden surge of gas through the tube creates a shock wave. The shock tube has produced temperatures as high as 23,000 degrees Celsius, but they last only a fraction of a second.

Standing Up under the Heat

In the furnaces of a steel mill, a temperature is reached

that is high enough to melt iron. The furnace, to be of any use, must be lined with a material that will not also melt when this temperature is reached. The same problem arises in the construction of a jet engine or a rocket engine. The materials used must be able to stand up under the high temperatures reached inside these engines. The problem has to be faced in designing the body of the rocket, too. When the rocket travels at supersonic speed, the shock wave it creates is very hot. Ways must be worked out of protecting the rocket from the heat flowing from the shock wave. This may be done by means of a cooling system in the body of the rocket, and by the use of special materials able to withstand high temperatures.

Materials that can stand up under high temperatures, without breaking or melting, are called *refractory materials*. Because of the great need for refractory materials, industry is constantly trying to develop new and better ones. For some purposes it uses alloys of iron produced by adding to it other metals like nickel, manganese, chromium, cobalt, molybdenum, tungsten, or columbium. Such alloys can withstand temperatures up to about 1000 degrees Celsius. In equipment that has to face higher temperatures, specially developed *ceramics* may be used. Ceramics are potterylike materials made of compounds in which metals are combined with oxygen, carbon, boron, or silicon. Some of these ceramics have melting points above 1700 degrees Celsius. To combine the strength of metals with the heat resistance of ceramics, some companies are now making mixtures of metals and ceramics. These mixtures are called *cermets*.

The Solar Furnace

As new materials are developed, they have to be tested before they are used. This is done by subjecting them to a high temperature in the laboratory. One way of producing the high temperatures needed is to use the solar furnace, a modern improvement of an old device. If you hold a magnifying glass in bright sunlight, it bends the rays of sunlight that fall on it, making them converge to a point. If you hold a piece of paper at this point, the concentrated rays make it hot enough to catch fire. A large magnifying glass catches more sunlight to concentrate than a small one does, so the larger the lens is, the higher the temperature that it can produce. A mirror curved in the shape of a headlight reflector can also concentrate the rays of the sun in the same way that a

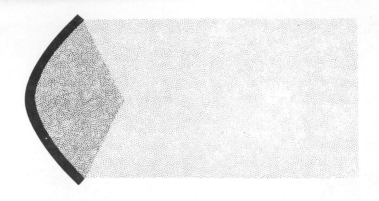

lens does. The National Bureau of Standards in Washington has made a solar furnace out of a curved mirror taken from an old army searchlight. The mirror catches the sun's rays that fall on a circle five feet wide, and concentrates them in a small spot a quarter of an inch wide. Materials to be tested are placed at this spot. The temperature reached there is about 3500 degrees Celsius.

Solar furnace with ten-foot mirror. *Convair*

Some ceramic materials tested in the solar furnace (from left to right):

Top row: Fused aluminum oxide, melting point 2030°C.; firebrick, melting point 1650°C.; zirconium dioxide, melting point 2700°C.

Center row: Graphite, melting point 3500°C.; boron nitride, melting point 3000°C.; pressed aluminum oxide, melting point 2030°C.

Bottom row: Boron nitride, melting point 3000°C.; aluminum magnesium silicate, melting point 1650°C.; magnesium oxide, melting point 2800°C. *Convair*

Electric Furnaces

An electric furnace takes advantage of the fact that an electric current produces heat. There are many types of electric furnace, depending on the purpose for which it is to be used. Some electric furnaces permit the current to pass through a special *resistance wire*, which becomes hot as the current flows through it. Then the object to be heated is held near the wire, to catch the heat as it flows or radiates away from the wire. Electric kitchen stoves and broilers are "furnaces" of this type. Resistance wires made of nickel-chromium alloys produce temperatures up to 1100 degrees Celsius. To reach temperatures above 1500 degrees Celsius, such metals as molybdenum, tungsten, and rhodium are used.

When the material heated is an ore from which metal is to be extracted, the material itself serves as part of the electric circuit of the furnace. An electric current is passed directly through the material to make it hot, entering the material at one terminal and leaving it at another. In some processes, after a compound is melted by the heat of the current, the current serves another purpose. It then separates the chemical elements that are in the compound, pulling them to opposite terminals. This is done, for example, when bauxite, an aluminum compound, is heated to remove the aluminum from it.

In one type of furnace, an electric current is made to flow through the material to be heated, even though the material is not made part of the electrical circuit of the furnace. This kind of furnace, known as an *induction furnace*, works the way a transformer does. In a transformer, two coils of wire are wound around an iron core. If a current is made to vibrate back and forth through one coil, called the *primary winding*, it makes a magnetic field vibrate back and forth in the space around it. The vibrating magnetic field then makes a current go back and forth in the second coil, called the *secondary*

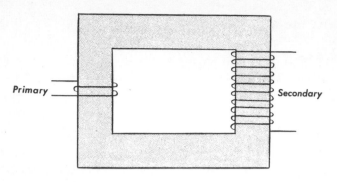

Transformer

winding. In the induction furnace, the object to be heated takes the place of the secondary winding. It has to be a good conductor of electricity. The vibrating magnetic field reaches out to the object from the primary winding in the furnace, and makes a current vibrate in it. Then the current makes it hot. The way in which the induction furnace works is demonstrated in a spectacular stunt that is part of a stage show one of the large electric companies has prepared for school assembly programs. The demonstrator holds a frying pan, with eggs in it, about a foot above the induction furnace. He also places one of his hands halfway between the frying pan and the furnace. While his hand remains cool and comfortable, the frying pan above it becomes hot, and the eggs begin to fry! The vibrating magnetic field of the furnace reaches out to both the hand and the frying pan. It makes a current flow in the frying pan because the metal of the pan is a good conductor. It causes no current in the hand because the hand is a very poor conductor. That is why the hand remains cool while the pan gets hot.

Ripping the Air

Very high temperature are produced in an *arc furnace* by making an electric current rip through the air. Two carbon rods, called *electrodes*, are placed opposite each other across an air gap, and are connected to a high-voltage source. The voltage compels electrons to leave one of the rods, and then pushes them toward the other. The rod that the electrons move away from is called the *cathode*. The other rod is called the *anode*. As the electrons rush away from the cathode, they actually tear the air. They collide with the molecules of air and tear electrons out of them. The electrons torn out of the atoms are pulled by the voltage, so they join the stream flowing toward the anode. The molecules from which electrons are torn become positive ions, and because of their electrical charge they are pushed by the voltage, too, and move in the opposite direction. They flow toward the cathode. Because the ripped air has large numbers of charged particles or ions in it, it is a plasma. Two streams of electric current are flowing in this plasma. One stream, made up of negative electrons, moves from the cathode to the anode. The other stream, made up of positive ions, moves the other way. There are many more collisions in the air, and these make the air

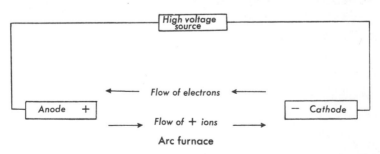

Arc furnace

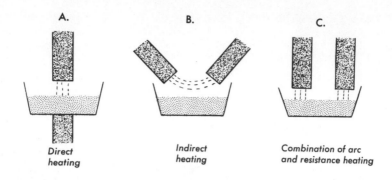

A. Direct heating

B. Indirect heating

C. Combination of arc and resistance heating

Ways of using an arc furnace

hotter. Now and then, when an electron passes close enough to a positive ion, it is attracted by it, and when it "falls" under the pull of the ion's charge, it releases a flash of light. There are many such flashes, so the whole plasma between the electrodes begins to glow. At this stage, the glowing current is called a *spark*. If the voltage is high enough, the stream of electrons striking the anode hits it hard enough to break some positive ions out of it. The new supply of ions reinforces the stream flowing toward the cathode. When this happens, the plasma becomes hotter and glows with a brilliant white light. In this second stage, the glowing current is called an *arc*. If the temperature of the arc goes above the boiling point of carbon, a large supply of ions is boiled out of the anode to make the current stronger and the temperature higher. In this third stage, the current is called a *high-intensity arc*. Arc temperatures range from 3400 to 4900 degrees Celsius. The high-intensity arc can reach 10,000 degrees Celsius.

Man's Highest Steady Temperature

The highest temperature man has been able to maintain for more than a fraction of a second is produced by a special kind of arc called a *plasma jet*. The furnace that makes the plasma jet is a partly closed cylinder. A carbon rod serves as an anode, and is mounted inside the cylinder at one end. The cathode is mounted on the opposite side, and has a hole through it. The plasma jet shoots away from the anode toward the cathode and passes through the hole, so it can be used for heating things that are outside the cylinder. While the furnace is operating, a stream of water or cold gas is sprayed into it through a special opening just above the anode. The cold spray cools the anode and protects it. It also cools the outer layer of the plasma that is nearest the wall of the

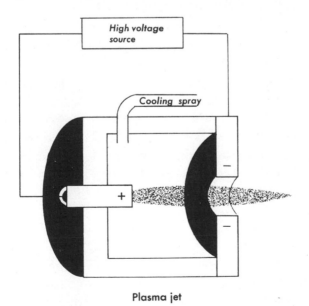

Plasma jet

cylinder. The cooled plasma becomes a poor conductor, and carries less of the current. As a result, the current is concentrated in the middle of the jet. The extra-strong current in the center of the jet produces an extra-high temperature. It also has another very important effect. An electric current is always surrounded by a field of magnetic force. The field pushes in against the current and squeezes it toward the center. This is called the *magnetic pinch effect*. Because of this pinch effect, the jet becomes narrower, the current in it becomes stronger, and the plasma becomes hotter. The plasma jet has produced temperatures as high as 14,500 degrees Celsius.

Cooking the Atom

One of the really important uses of high temperature is to "cook" hydrogen atoms in what is called the *thermonuclear* reaction. If nuclei of heavy hydrogen are thrown at each other with great force, they can be made to fuse to form helium, releasing a large amount of energy at the same time. The way to make hydrogen nuclei strike each other with great force is to make the plasma that contains them very hot. Then the nuclei dash about at great speed, and many of them collide with each other. One way of making the plasma hot enough to start the thermonuclear reaction is to place it at the center of an atomic bomb explosion. The explosion produces a temperature of about 55 million degrees Celsius. This high temperature lasts less than a millionth of a second, but that is enough time to throw the hydrogen nuclei together to make them fuse. Then the fusion produces another explosion, even larger than the atomic bomb explosion. The device that produces a thermonuclear reaction in this way is called a hydrogen bomb.

The fusion of hydrogen nuclei in the explosion of a hydrogen bomb produces so much energy all at once that it destroys everything around it for miles. If we could only get the fusion to take place slowly, releasing only a little energy at a time, we could capture this energy and put it to use. Scientists are now searching for ways of making the fusion take place slowly in what they call a *controlled* thermonuclear reaction. One way in which they hope to produce controlled fusion is by heating a plasma of heavy hydrogen by passing an electric current through it. One of the difficult problems they face arises from the fact that a plasma that is hot enough to cause hydrogen nuclei to fuse is also hot enough to vaporize the container that holds the plasma. To avoid this difficulty, they must try to keep the plasma away from the walls of the container when the plasma is hot. They are relying on the magnetic pinch effect to do this for them. In all the attempts to produce controlled fusion, the plasma that is being heated is enclosed in a long tube. When the current through the plasma becomes strong, the pinch effect squeezes it toward the center of the tube, away from the walls. In the tubes known as *stellarators*, used in thermonuclear experiments at Princeton University, coils twisted around the tubes produce an additional magnetic force to help push the plasma toward the center.

The invention of the *laser* has opened up the possibility of producing controlled fusion in another way. A laser is a device that produces a very powerful beam of light that is all of one wave length, with all the waves in step so that they reinforce each other. Since a laser beam can be

Stellarator tubes. *Project Matterhorn*

focused very sharply, it can be used to concentrate a large amount of energy in a small space and produce a very high temperature there. If the temperature can be made as high as 50 million degrees Celsius, it would be capable of fusing heavy hydrogen.

Scientists at Oak Ridge National Laboratory have designed a laser-beam reactor which they hope will be able to produce energy by fusion. The principal parts of the reactor are a spherical tank, a lithium pump, and a

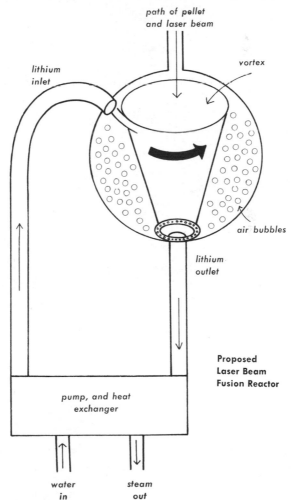

path of pellet
and laser beam

vortex

lithium
inlet

air bubbles

lithium
outlet

Proposed
Laser Beam
Fusion Reactor

pump, and heat
exchanger

water
in

steam
out

heat exchanger. The reactor will work in this way: Liquid lithium, pushed by the the lithium pump, will flow into the tank at the top at high speed. The lithium will flow in sideways, so that it will swirl around inside the tank as it flows to the drainpipe at the bottom, forming a vortex the way water flowing out of a bathtub does. Meanwhile air bubbles will be flowing into the lithium through holes in a ring at the bottom of the tank. The fuel for the reactor will be frozen pellets of heavy hydrogen. A pellet will be thrown into the vortex through an opening at the top of the tank. When the pellet reaches the center of the tank, it will be hit by a laser beam that will also come in from the top. If the reactor works as planned, the beam will raise the temperature of the pellet to more than 50 million degrees Celsius. The heavy hydrogen atoms will fuse to form an explosion of helium atoms and neutrons carrying a large amount of energy. The bubbles in the lithium will serve as shock absorbers to cushion the explosion. The lithium will be heated by the energy of the explosion, so that its temperature will rise a few hundred degrees in a millionth of a second. The heated lithium, flowing out of the drainpipe of the tank, will go to a heat-exchanger, where heat, flowing from the lithium to water, will turn the water into steam. The cooled lithium will go on to the lithium pump which will force it into the top of the tank again.

CHAPTER VI

From Icebox to Cryostat

THERE ARE many occasions when we purposely make things colder than they are. At home, we put food into the refrigerator to chill it so that it will not spoil. We allow freshly cooked food to stand until it cools so that it will not burn us when we eat it. In the hospital, a doctor will sometimes freeze a small area of a patient's flesh so that he may cut into it in an operation without causing pain. In the chemical industry, it is sometimes necessary to grind delicate compounds like vitamins and hormones. Grinding them produces heat, and too much heat would destroy them. So the manufacturer freezes them first before he grinds them. Then they do not get too hot, and are not destroyed. In the laboratory a scientist studying the behavior of molecules may bring their temperature down close to absolute zero so that they will not jump around too much while he studies them. Other scientists produce low temperatures merely to see what happens when they do. Some strange things happen near absolute zero, and learning about them gives us a better understanding of the nature of the world we live in. There are many different ways of making things cold. This chapter describes the most important ones by which, step by step, man gradually pushed temperatures lower and lower, to reach a temperature that is only a hundred-thousandth of a degree Kelvin above absolute zero.

Cooling by Radiation

The simplest way to cool something, if it is hotter than the things that surround it, is to leave it alone. Every hot body loses energy by sending out heat rays. It also gains energy by receiving heat rays from the things that surround it. But hot bodies radiate more heat than cooler bodies. So the hot body will lose more energy than it gains, and will gradually cool off until its temperature is the same as that of the bodies around it. When we allow a hot dish of food to stand until it cools, this is the method of cooling that we use. We cannot produce very low temperatures by this method. While it helps us make exceptionally hot things as cool as its neighbors, it cannot be used to make a body colder than its neighbors.

Conducting Heat Away

Another simple way to make something cool is to place it next to a body that has a lower temperature. Then heat flows from the warmer body to the colder one. In the old-fashioned icebox, we cooled food by placing it on a cake of ice whose temperature was 273 degrees Kelvin. Today, when baby's bottle is too hot, mother may cool it by putting it into a dish of cold water whose temperature is about 283 degrees Kelvin. The manufacturer who wants to freeze vitamins before grinding them will cool them in a bath of liquid nitrogen whose temperature is about 78 degrees Kelvin. A scientist, working at temperatures near absolute zero, may cool things off in his cryostat (a low-temperature refrigerator) by bathing them in liquid helium, whose temperature is about 4 degrees Kelvin.

Cooling by Evaporating a Liquid

Energy is used up when a liquid is turned into vapor. So, when a liquid evaporates, it is continually losing energy with the molecules that leave it to become vapor. Its temperature falls. Then, when it is cooler than neighboring bodies, it begins to draw heat from them by conduction and radiation. So an evaporating liquid can be used to make other bodies cool. This is the principle we rely on in the modern refrigerator. A liquid that evaporates easily (called a *refrigerant*) flows through pipes in the refrigerator. As part of the refrigerant evaporates in the pipes, the rest of it becomes cold and withdraws heat from the air and food in the refrigerator. More and more of the refrigerant evaporates, and the vapor flows through the pipes to a compressor. The compressor squeezes the vapor and turns it into liquid again. When the refrigerant is compressed, it warms up. As the warmer liquid refrigerant flows away from the compressor, it moves through pipes exposed to the air outside the refrigerator. It loses heat to the air before returning to the pipes inside the refrigerator in which it evaporates again. In this way, the heat withdrawn from the food inside the refrigerator is transferred to the air outside.

101

An evaporating liquid is sometimes used as an anesthetic or painkiller in surgery. If a doctor has to lance a boil, he may first spray it with ethyl chloride, a liquid that evaporates very easily. As it evaporates, it withdraws heat from the boil and the flesh around it, and freezes it. The quick-frozen flesh is numb and does not feel pain when the doctor cuts into it with his lance.

The principle of cooling by evaporation is used at very low temperatures, too. When the gas helium is liquefied, its temperature at first is 4.2 degrees Kelvin. If some of the liquid is allowed to evaporate under low pressure, the liquid that remains behind can be cooled to a temperature as low as 1 degree Kelvin.

Cooling by Expanding a Gas

When a gas is compressed, it becomes warm. If the gas is allowed to expand, the opposite happens. It becomes cool. When the gas expands, it moves from a smaller space into a larger space. The gas grows cool because some of its thermal energy is changed into energy of motion. This is the principle behind the methods used for cooling a gas down to its boiling point to liquefy it. The diagram opposite shows in simplified form the steps by which ordinary air is turned into a liquid. First, air is admitted to the compressor. Then it is compressed into a small space. When it is compressed, it grows warmer. The compressed air flows away from the compressor through a pipe that passes through a water jacket. Cold water, flowing through the coils of the water jacket, removes some heat from the compressed air. The air continues flowing through the pipe to a nozzle that opens into the expansion chamber. There the air expands, cooling as it does so. Then it flows through the return pipe to the compression chamber. The air in the return pipe flows over the pipe that is carrying air to the expansion chamber. So the air that has already cooled by expanding helps to cool the air that is about to be expanded. After returning to the compression chamber, it goes through the cycle again and again. Its temperature is reduced step by step until it reaches the point of liquefaction (the boiling point of liquid air). Then drops of liquid begin to form, and collect in the bottom of the expansion chamber.

Liquid air is a mixture of two liquefied gases, liquid nitrogen and liquid oxygen. (There are other gases in it, too, but they make up only a minute fraction of the whole.) The boiling point of liquid nitrogen is about 78 degrees Kelvin. The boiling point of liquid oxygen is about 90 degrees Kelvin. The difference in boiling points makes it possible to separate the two liquids from each other. If the liquid air is allowed to warm up to a temperature of 78 degrees Kelvin, the nitrogen begins to boil out of the liquid, while the oxygen does not. The nitrogen vapor can be caught and liquefied again, to make pure

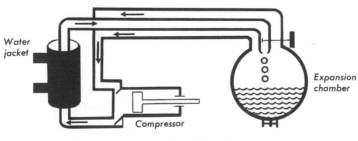

Water jacket

Expansion chamber

Compressor

Liquefying air

liquid nitrogen. When all the nitrogen is boiled out of the liquid air, what remains is practically pure liquid oxygen.

The first time that a gas was cooled to its boiling point by expansion was in 1834, when carbon dioxide was liquefied by this method. As the years went by, scientists succeeded in reaching lower and lower temperatures until finally, in 1908, helium, the gas with the lowest boiling point (4.2 degrees Kelvin), was liquefied for the first time by the Dutch scientist H. K. Onnes. With the temperature of 4.2 degrees as the starting point, it was then possible to cool the helium to 1 degree Kelvin above absolute zero by evaporating some of it under low pressure.

Magnetic Cooling

Before 1933, the lowest temperature ever reached was 1 degree Kelvin. In that year scientists broke through to temperatures below 1 degree by using a new method proposed by Giauque and Debye. The new method takes advantage of the magnetic properties of certain salts known as *paramagnetic* salts.

In every atom, the electrons that surround the nucleus are spinning like tops. This motion of the electrons is like a tiny electric current, so it produces a magnetic field, making a small magnet out of each spinning electron. Each of these little magnets is like a bar magnet, with a north pole and a south pole. In a paramagnetic salt, these little magnets behave as though they have no effect on each other. While one magnet points in one direction, its neighbors may point in other directions. As a result, the magnets are tilted in a disordered way, as shown in

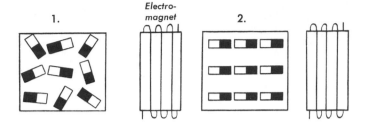

1.　**Electro-magnet**　**2.**

diagram 1. If an electromagnet is brought near the salt, the pull of the electromagnet swings all the little magnets around until they are lined up in an orderly way, as shown in diagram 2. When this happens, we say that the salt has been magnetized. Theory and experiment both show that when the salt is magnetized, it becomes warmer. When the electromagnet is removed, the process is reversed. The salt becomes demagnetized. The little atomic magnets become disordered again, and the salt grows cooler. The cooling that occurs when the salt is demagnetized is used to reach temperatures below 1 degree Kelvin.

Here is how it is done. The salt is mounted in the center of a container that is filled with helium gas. The container itself is surrounded by a bath of liquid helium, kept at a temperature of 1 degree Kelvin. Heat flows freely through the helium gas from the salt to the liquid helium bath, so the salt cools down until its temperature, too, is 1 degree Kelvin. An electromagnet is brought near, and the salt is magnetized. The salt becomes warmer as a result, but then its extra thermal energy flows away as heat through the helium gas to the liquid helium until its temperature is reduced again to 1 degree Kelvin. Then the helium gas is pumped out of the

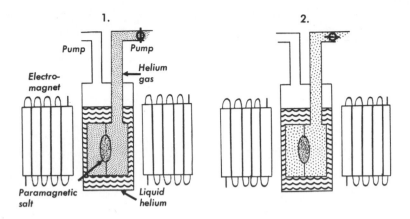

1.

Pump

Electro-
magnet

Pump

Helium
gas

Paramagnetic
salt

Liquid
helium

When the salt is magnetized, the heat
released flows to the liquid helium.

2.

The helium gas
is pumped out

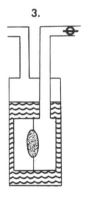

3.

When the salt is demagnetized,
it grows colder.

Magnetic cooling

container. Next, the electromagnet is removed. The salt becomes demagnetized and grows cooler, so its temperature falls below 1 degree Kelvin. Now the liquid helium bath is warmer than the salt, but no heat flows back from the bath to the salt because the helium gas, through which it might have flowed, has been removed. By this method of demagnetizing a paramagnetic salt, it is possible to reach a temperature only one-thousandth of a degree Kelvin above absolute zero.

In 1956, lower temperatures were reached by the British scientist Kurti by using a refinement of this method. In metallic copper there are disordered little magnets, too. But these magnets result from the spinning of the nuclei of the atoms rather than from the spinning of the electrons. The nuclear magnets are one thousand times weaker than the electronic magnets. This difference in strength makes it possible to use them to reach lower temperatures. By magnetizing the copper, drawing off the extra heat, and then demagnetizing it, the copper can be cooled. The copper is in contact with a paramagnetic salt. First the salt is cooled to a temperature of one-thousandth of a degree Kelvin by the method described above. The cold salt is used to cool the copper. When the copper is magnetized, the heat released in it is withdrawn by the salt and passed on to a liquid helium bath. Then, when the copper is demagnetized, it becomes cooler than the paramagnetic salt. By nuclear magnetic cooling it is possible to reach a temperature only one hundred-thousandth of a degree Kelvin above absolute zero.

The Helium 3 / Helium 4 Dilution Process

Helium is a mixture of two different kinds of helium molecules that are the same chemically, but have different weights. One of them, known as Helium 3, is about three times as heavy as an ordinary hydrogen atom. The other one, known as Helium 4, is four times as heavy as a hydrogen atom. This fact plays a part in a new method of cooling that can produce a steady temperature of only one-hundredth of a degree Kelvin.

In this method, liquid helium is first cooled to a temperature of eight-tenths of a degree Kelvin. At this temperature, the helium begins to separate into two layers, with the upper layer made up mostly of Helium 3, which is lighter than Helium 4. As the temperature falls some more, the separation continues until, at a temperature of five-hundredths of a degree Kelvin, the upper layer is practically pure Helium 3, while the lower layer has about 6 percent Helium 3 dissolved in the Helium 4 (six parts Helium 3 in every hundred parts). Then, after this, a new process begins to take effect. The molecules of Helium 3 in the upper layer are moving about at different speeds, some faster than others. The faster ones tend to escape from the upper layer into the lower layer. As a result, the average speed of the molecules that remain in the upper layer falls, and with it, the average kinetic energy of the molecules in this layer also falls. But the temperature is a measure of this average kinetic energy. So, as the faster molecules of Helium 3 escape from the upper layer of helium, the temperature of this layer falls.

The Pomeranchuk Method

Between 1965 and 1969, American and Russian physicists developed and improved another system for producing low temperatures, based on a method first proposed in 1950 by the Russian scientist Pomeranchuk. The method takes advantage of a peculiar property of Helium 3: If liquid Helium 3 is compressed into a solid when its temperature is above 318-thousandths of a degree Kelvin, the temperature rises. But if the temperature is below 318-thousandths of a degree Kelvin when the Helium 3 is compressed, then the temperature falls. So, when the temperature of liquid Helium 3 is below 318-thousandths of a degree Kelvin, it can be made even lower by compressing the liquid into a solid. A temperature of two-thousandths of a degree Kelvin can be reached in this way.

Strange Doings Near Absolute Zero

After H. K. Onnes succeeded in liquefying helium, he began to use it to make other materials very cold so that he could see how they behave at very low temperatures. He discovered that when some metals are made cold enough, they suddenly become *superconductors* of electricity. In the normal state, at ordinary temperatures, one of these metals behaves the way all metals do, and resists the flow of an electric current through it. If an electric current is launched in a ring made of the metal, the resistance changes the electrical energy into heat, and the current dies out. But when the metal is in the super-conducting state, it has *no resistance at all.* If a current is started in a superconducting ring, since there is no resistance to interfere with it, the current keeps flowing indefinitely, as long as the ring is kept cold. If it is allowed to warm up, its resistance is restored, and the current dies out. A current in a superconducting ring of lead will flow for years without any signs of weakening. In one experiment with superconductivity, a ball of lead was made to hang in space inside a cylinder without any visible support. Beneath the ball, but not touching it, was a lead ring. The ball and the ring were being kept cool by a liquid helium bath surrounding the cylinder, so that both were superconductors. Electric currents had been started in the ball and the ring, and these currents made them both magnets. The magnetic force acting between the ball and the ring pushed them apart, and kept the ball hanging above the ring.

Physicists have been testing the metals one by one, to see which metals can become superconductors and to find out how cold they must be to acquire this strange property. They found that the metals that become super-conductors at the highest temperatures are those whose atoms have 3, 5, or 7 electrons in the outermost layer of electrons surrounding the nucleus. Technetium, for example, which has seven electrons in the outer layer of each of its atoms, becomes superconducting at the "high" temperature of 11 degrees Kelvin. They also found that the best superconductors are those metals in whose crystals the atoms are arranged in groups of eight to form cubes. These discoveries suggested a way of making new superconductors. If different metals are mixed in the right amounts, it is sometimes possible to get the atoms to cluster together in groups of eight to form cubes while the average number of electrons in the outer layers within the atoms averages 3, 5, or 7. Under these conditions, the mixture becomes a superconductor more easily than the separate metals that are in it. For example, molybdenum does not become a superconductor at all, even if it is cooled to one-tenth of a degree Kelvin. But molybdenum mixed with tin in the right amounts becomes a superconductor at 18 degrees Kelvin. There is also an alloy of niobium, aluminum and germanium that becomes a superconductor at a temperature of 21 degrees Kelvin. This is a temperature that is high enough to maintain with ease, so we shall soon see superconductors used in industry.

Superconducting Magnets

The existence of superconducting metals opens the way to making electromagnets that will be able to produce a strong magnetic field while using up only a small amount of electrical power.

A permanent iron magnet produces a magnetic field without using any electrical power at all. But the field of a permanent magnet is not very strong. Its greatest strength is about 10,000 gauss. An electromagnet can produce a stronger magnetic field, but it must be supplied with electrical power to maintain the field. A conventional electromagnet can produce a magnetic field that is twenty-five times as strong as that of a permanent iron magnet. But to do so, it must be supplied with 16 million watts of electrical power, enough to serve a town of 15,000 people. The advantage of a superconducting magnet is that, once it starts working, no electrical power is needed to keep an electric current flowing through it, because there is no electrical resistance in it that has to be overcome. The only power used by a superconducting magnet is the power used to build up the magnetic field in the first place, and the power used to cool the conducting material to the temperature at which it becomes superconducting. Superconducting magnets have been made that can produce a magnetic field that is fourteen times as strong as that of a permanent iron magnet.

The Cryotron

A superconductor is a metal whose electrical resistance has been destroyed by cooling. It stops being a superconductor when its resistance has been restored. This can be done in two ways. One way is to allow the metal to get warmer. The other way is to surround the metal with a magnetic field. If the field is strong enough, the metal regains its resistance. The second method is used in the *cryotron*, a new device for controlling the flow of electric current. In the cryotron, a coil of niobium is wound around a wire made of tantalum. The metals are cooled by liquid helium to the point where they are both superconducting. If a current flows through the tantalum wire, it can be controlled by a current flowing through the niobium coil. The current through the coil makes it a magnet. If the magnetic field it creates is strong enough, the resistance of the tantalum is restored, and the current through the tantalum dies out. The cryotron will soon join the vacuum tube and the transistor in the controls of automatic machinery.

A Heat Valve

When lead becomes a superconductor of electricity, it also becomes a very poor conductor of heat. This fact makes it possible to use lead as a heat valve that allows heat to flow in only one direction. At Ohio State University, such a heat valve was built into a cryostat that can cool things to a temperature of three-tenths of a degree Kelvin. The schematic diagram below shows how it works. The material that has to be cooled is joined by a piece of lead (marked valve #1) to a paramagnetic salt. The salt is connected by another piece of lead (marked valve #2) to a liquid helium bath. The whole assembly is cold enough so that if no magnetic field is present across the lead, the lead is superconducting. Now

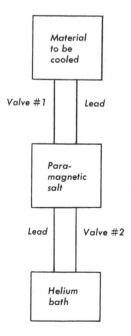

a one-way flow of heat out of the material to be cooled into the helium bath is produced in this way. A magnetic field is applied to valve #2, but not to valve #1. Valve #2 stops being a superconductor for electricity, but in its normal state it is a good conductor of heat, so it is "open" to the flow of heat. Valve #1, on the other hand, while it is a superconductor for electricity, is a very poor conductor of heat. So it is "closed" to the flow of heat. Now the paramagnetic salt is magnetized. It releases heat and the heat flows through the open valve #2 into the helium bath. Next the magnetic field is removed from valve #2, and is placed across valve #1. Now valve #1 is open to the

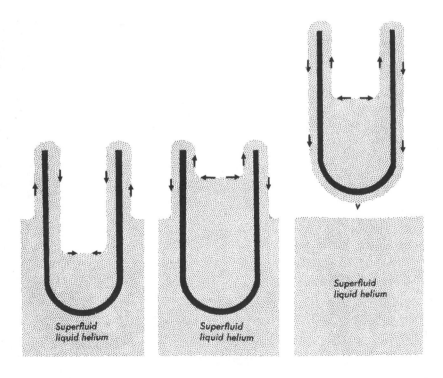

flow of heat, while valve #2 is closed. Then the salt is de-magnetized. It grows cooler as a result and draws heat through the open valve #1 from the material that has to be cooled. This chain of steps is repeated over and over again, each time removing a little more heat from the material and passing it on to the helium bath.

The Liquid That Climbs Walls

In 1937, the Russian scientist Kapitza discovered some more strange doings at temperatures near absolute zero. This time, the material that misbehaved was not a metal, but liquid helium itself. Kapitza found that when helium is cooled below 2.2 degrees Kelvin, it suddenly develops an unusual *superfluidity* that allows it to flow in the strangest places and in the strangest ways. If two polished glass plates are held a half micron (two hundred-thousandths of an inch) apart, the gap between them is so narrow that normal liquid helium cannot squeeze through it. But supercooled, superfluid helium flows through the gap easily as if it were a wide-open passageway. If the bottom of an empty flask is pushed part way into a bath of normal liquid helium, nothing unusual happens. The helium stays in the bath, and the flask remains empty. But if the bath consists of superfluid helium, the helium begins to climb up the wall of the flask to its mouth, and then down into the flask, until the level of the helium in the flask is the same as the level of the helium in the bath. If a flask that is nearly full of superfluid helium is dipped part way into the bath, the opposite happens. The helium climbs up out of the flask and glides down into the bath until the levels are equalized. If the flask is held above the bath, the helium climbs up over the mouth of the flask, glides down the sides, and drips down into the bath until the flask is empty.

Superfluid helium is also an unusually good conductor of heat. The best conductor of heat at ordinary temperatures is copper. But superfluid helium conducts heat 200 times as fast as copper normally does.

On Toward Absolute Zero

At the time this book is being written, the lowest temperature ever reached by man is one hundred-thousandth of a degree Kelvin. There can be no doubt that in a few years, with the stronger electromagnets that are being built, the method of magnetic cooling will take us even closer to absolute zero. Will we ever reach absolute zero? Physical theory tells us we shall not. Laboratory experience also shows us that the closer we get to absolute zero, the more difficult it becomes to get still closer. But scientists will keep pushing temperatures down and down, turning up more puzzles like superconductivity and superfluidity, and then solving them. Their studies lead us to new facts about liquids and solids, a better understanding of their behavior, and new useful devices like cryostats and cryotrons.

CHAPTER VII

The Earth's Heat

A Giant Heat Engine

THE EARTH is a great heat engine in which thermal energy is converted into energy of motion. The motion produced by this heat engine includes the movements of continents, oceans and the atmosphere, and that delicate, complicated form of motion that we call life. We shall look briefly at the workings of this heat engine both inside the earth and at its surface.

The Temperature Inside the Earth

Deep inside the earth the temperature is higher than it is at the surface. This is shown by several familiar facts: 1) When a volcano erupts, hot molten lava (melted rock) rises up from inside the earth. The temperature of this lava is about 1100 degrees Celsius. 2) In some places there are hot springs, where hot water rises out of the earth. At these springs the temperature of the ground increases with depth very sharply, increasing several hundred degrees Celsius in a few hundred feet of depth. 3) In mines, the temperature also increases with depth. In the gold mines of South Africa, some of which are as deep as 9000 feet, the temperature increases 1 degree

Celsius for every 300 feet of depth. From these facts, and from other information that they have, geologists estimate that on the average the temperature inside the earth increases about 32 degrees Celsius for every mile of depth, down to a depth of about 30 miles. Below that the rate of increase is probably smaller. The temperature at the center of the earth may be between 2000 and 3000 degrees Celsius.

What Made the Earth Hot

Why is the earth so hot inside? The answer to this question given by scientists is based on a theory of how the earth was formed, and a fact about what has been going on in the earth since it was formed. The theory is that the earth was formed about four thousand million years ago by the contraction of a swirling mass of gas, dust and small particles in space. The mass contracted because each part of it was pulled toward every other part by the force of gravitation. As the mass contracted, gravitational energy was released, first in the form of kinetic energy. Then as the particles collided, the kinetic energy was gradually changed into thermal energy, with the temperature rising as the average speed of the disorderly motion of the molecules in the earth increased. The fact is that some of the atoms inside the earth, like uranium, thorium and some potassium, are radioactive. They break up spontaneously and release energy as they do so. This has been going on for the four thousand million years that the earth has existed. The energy released by radioactive atoms has also helped to raise the temperature inside the earth.

118

Movement Inside the Earth

Because the earth is hotter at the center than it is at the surface, there is a steady flow of heat outward from the center. There is also a circulation of hot lava just as there is a circulation of hot air near a stove. This circulation is responsible for the cracking of the ocean floor and for a slow drifting of the continents. It plays a part in the formation of mountains, and it causes earthquakes and volcanic eruptions.

Heat Flow at the Surface

The earth, like any hot body, loses heat by radiation from its surface. However, at the same time, the earth also receives radiant heat from the sun. The heat it receives makes up for the heat that it loses.

The flow of heat at the surface of the earth comes from several sources. Heat flows up from the inside by conduction at the rate of about 110 million million BTUs per hour. Additional heat is carried up by the flow of hot water or lava in hot springs and volcanoes at the rate of about 1 million million BTUs per hour. The movement of the tides, caused by the pull of the sun and the moon, adds some more energy at the rate of 10 million million BTUs per hour. But all this flow of energy is swamped by the flow of radiant energy from the sun. Energy from the sun falls on the surface of the earth at the rate of about 600,000 million million BTUs per hour. This is five thousand times as great as the energy flow to the surface from all other sources combined.

If all the energy flowing in from the sun stayed on the

earth, the earth would be getting hotter and hotter. But this does not happen. Out of every 100 parts of the energy that reaches the earth from the sun, 30 parts are immediately reflected back to space by the continents, the oceans and the clouds above them. Another 23 parts are converted into energy of movement. Only 47 parts are converted into thermal energy, and then they share in the outward flow of radiation from the earth.

Movement at the Surface of the Earth

About a quarter of the energy that the earth receives from the sun (23 parts out of 100) is converted into energy of motion. It moves the water in the ocean in ocean currents and the air in the atmosphere in winds. It moves water into the air from the ocean by evaporation, ultimately causing rain, and the flow of rivers down to the sea.

The Energy of Life

A tiny fraction of the energy the earth receives from the sun is captured by plants. It is only one-thousandth of the amount that is changed into energy of motion. But it is a large amount of energy nevertheless, equal to about 136 million million BTUs per hour. The plants store this energy in the food that they manufacture. This stored energy supplies the energy of life of the plants and the animals that feed on them.

Unequal Heating, Climate and Weather

Different parts of the earth receive different amounts of the sunlight that reaches the earth. The smallest share of the sunlight reaches the regions around the north and south poles. The largest share of the sunlight reaches the region around the equator. For this reason, the ground at the equator is warmer than at the poles. The air, warmed at the equator, rises, and then high above the ground, it moves away from the equator toward the north and south poles. It sinks again about one-third of the way to the poles, and returns to the equator along the ground, thus completing a full cycle of movement. At the poles, the opposite movement takes place. The air sinks to the ground from aloft, and then moves away from the poles toward the equator. About one-third of the way to the equator it has warmed up enough to rise again, and it returns to the pole high up above the ground, completing a second cycle of movement. Between these two cycles there is a third one, as shown in the diagram, in which the air near the ground moves toward the pole, and the air aloft moves toward the equator.

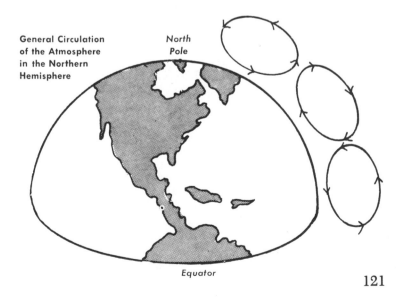

General Circulation of the Atmosphere in the Northern Hemisphere

North Pole

Equator

The unequal heating of the equator and the poles is a chief cause of the differences in climate between the polar and equatorial regions. The three cycles of air movement that result from this unequal heating are the main cause of the prevailing winds. Seasonal and daily changes in the unequal heating of the earth's surface account for the daily changes in weather.*

Geothermal Power

Nearly all the power used to heat homes and run factories is obtained by burning coal, oil and gas. Oil and gas from oil wells are being burned up so fast that there is a growing shortage of these fuels, and they will probably be all used up by the year 2000. This makes it necessary for us to find other power sources to take their place. One that will be used more and more in the next few years is *geothermal power*, obtained by putting to work some of the thermal energy stored in hot magma inside the earth.

There are many places around the world where underground water is very hot. The water is heated by the rocks there, and the rocks draw their heat from the hot magma that surrounds them. In some of these places the water has been changed to steam at a very high temperature and pressure. These are called "dry" steam fields. In others, the water is still in liquid form but, at high underground pressure, is superheated to temperatures ranging from 350 to 700 degrees Fahrenheit. When the water is brought to the surface where the pressure is lower, the superheated water becomes steam. These places are

*For more details about weather, see *Weather in Your Life*, by the same author. New York, The John Day Company, 1959.

called "wet" steam fields. Steam drawn from a steam field can be used to turn the turbines of an electric power plant.

The first geothermal power plant was built in Italy in 1904. Others have since been built in Japan, Hungary, the U.S.S.R., the United States, Iceland, New Zealand and other places.

A particularly interesting geothermal plant, being developed in Chile with the help of the United Nations, will serve three different purposes: it will produce energy, fresh water and valuable minerals. A mixture of steam and brine is brought up from under the ground where its temperature is 450 degrees Fahrenheit. The steam and brine are then separated. The steam is used to

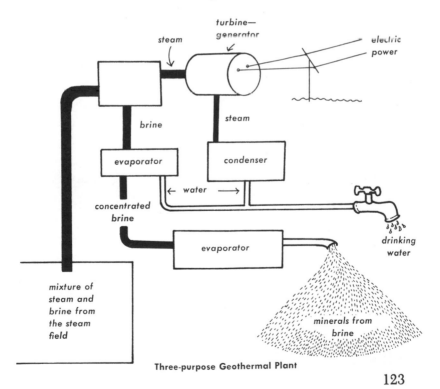

Three-purpose Geothermal Plant

generate electrical power. The water in the brine is removed by evaporation. The steam and some of the evaporated water are condensed to provide pure drinking water. After all the water of the brine is evaporated, what is left is a mixture of minerals.

Heat and Life

What we call "life" is a complicated interlocking set of chemical reactions in which energy is released. This delicately balanced chemical activity can take place only within a narrow range of temperatures, between 32 degrees and 122 degrees Fahrenheit. There are animals that can survive at both extremes. The Alaskan stonefly lives normally at freezing temperatures. The fish *Barbus thermalis* lives at a temperature of 122 degrees Fahrenheit in hot springs in Ceylon. Some bacteria can survive beyond these extremes. Some, when cooled below freezing, stop all life activities, but can resume them when they are warmed up again. Others, found in deep oil-well brines, can live at a temperature of 212 degrees Fahrenheit.

The air or water in which animals live changes in temperature from hour to hour and from season to season. The animal world has evolved several ways of dealing with these changes. One way, used by the so-called "cold-blooded" animals, is to change the body temperature in step with the changes in the temperature of the surrounding air or water. Another way, used by the "warm-blooded" animals, is to maintain a steady body temperature even while the outside temperature changes. Man, for example, keeps a body temperature of about 99 degrees Fahrenheit. Songbirds maintain a temperature of nearly 113 degrees Fahrenheit. Some animals like the bear, live through cold winter temperatures by hibernation, a condition in which all life processes are slowed down.

Thermal Pollution

Fish are cold-blooded animals. They cool off when the water in which they live cools off. They warm up when the water warms up. But if the water gets too warm, the fish die. A temperature of 77 degrees Fahrenheit will kill trout. A temperature of 93 degrees Fahrenheit will kill nearly all fish. This means that water can be polluted not only by poisonous chemicals but also by heat. To keep our lakes and streams fit for fish to live in, we must be careful not to dump too much heat into them.

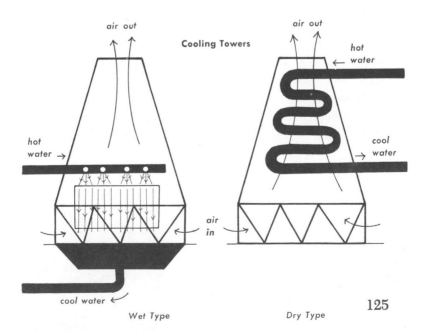

Cooling Towers

Wet Type   Dry Type

Preventing heat pollution is rapidly becoming a serious problem. In many industries, water is used for removing heat from things. The warmed-up water is then dumped into lakes or rivers. Nuclear power plants, which are now being built in increasing numbers, will produce a large amount of waste heat in the future. By the year 2000, the power industry in the United States will have to get rid of 20,000 million million BTUs of waste heat per day.

To protect the fish living in lakes and streams, it will be necessary to develop ways of removing most of this thermal energy from the water that carries it before the water enters the lakes or streams. The solution to this problem is to cool the water off in artificial cooling lakes and in cooling towers.

There are two different types of cooling tower. In the "wet" type, the hot water comes out into the open air, and it is cooled in two ways: 1) it passes some heat to the air; 2) it uses some to evaporate part of the water. This type has the disadvantage that it creates a fog in cool weather. In the "dry" type, the hot water does not come out into the open air. It merely flows through an air-cooled pipe, like the water in an automobile radiator. This type has the disadvantage of being very expensive. However, one type or the other will have to be used more and more as we continue to produce more and more heat in industry and in power plants in the years to come.

Index

127